What Leaders Are Saying

"My dear friend Steve Sampson has done a thorough and marvelous job of taking you step by step through the process of recognizing and unlearning the unhealthy and unaffirming behaviors of passivity and aggression. He also shows you the way into a life filled with the peace of God that passes all understanding and the joy that is your birthright in Christ. Steve effectively uses the templates of Ahab and Jezebel to personify these extremes in behavior, applying simple truths from Scripture to show you instead how to live assertively, the way Jesus lived."

— from the foreword by **Bishop Mark J. Chironna**, Ph.D., The Master's Touch International Church (Orlando, Florida); www.markchironna.com

"Steve Sampson shares with us on a critical issue for all believers in this hour. We have passively withdrawn from the battle again and again, and our children and this nation have suffered from the consequences of the Ahab spirit. May God use the insights in this book to help us take back the high places and release once again the Spirit of Elijah."

—**Mahesh Chavda**, senior pastor, All Nations Church (Charlotte, NC, and Atlanta, GA); www.maheshchavda.com

"With personal experiences to back him up, Steve Sampson shines light on the two emotions that control our lives: fear and love. Taking two characters from the Bible, Ahab and Jezebel, Steve uses these personality types to show how aggression and passivity can harm future relationships and your walk with God. With insight and passion, he reveals the key to overcoming both to live a fruitful and high-quality life with God at the center.

"Presently one of the principalities suffocating the spiritual resources of many nations is the Ahab spirit. Steve's book will definitely enlighten and assist you in your walk with God, and show you how to deal with these wicked spiritual forces."

—**Kim Clement**, author, *Call Me Crazy but I'm Hearing God* and *Secrets of the Prophetic*; www.kimclement.com

"I have known Steve Sampson for more than two decades. He has an unusual ability to unlock spiritual paradigms of behavior that are often seen in the lives of many Christians.

"When we first met in 1985, he was immediately embraced by the Covenant Church family for his sincerity and transparency. He has this marvelous ability for self-deprecation, enabling almost anyone to identify with his message. He takes complex truths and simplifies them for everyone listening. I have long admired his insight into Scripture with a view toward producing practical insights for his listeners and readers.

"Much has been said, taught and disseminated about the Jezebel spirit, but the polar opposite, the Ahab spirit, has remained hidden—until now. I believe this book will be a textbook for pastors, teachers and counselors to help people grow in their spiritual lives. And any Christian will benefit invaluably by Steve's wisdom."

—**Bishop Joseph L. Garlington Sr.**, Ph.D., senior pastor,
Covenant Church of Pittsburgh; www.ccop.org

"Steve Sampson has been given a unique prophetic anointing and is setting the captives free. His book *Confronting Jezebel* brought me life on every page. The illumination and insight caused the darkness around me to flee. Now he is giving us this new work that will continue where *Confronting Jezebel* left off, arming us with true revelation from God's Word."

—**Dr. Joe VanKoevering**, host, *God's News Behind the News*;
www.godsnews.com

"This book will not help you unless you read it! If you read it, you will have a guide for change and maturity that really works and will help you enjoy your Christian faith more. It is a bare-knuckled approach to the personal, social and spirit forces that alter or control our everyday lives. With love, grace and experience from years of ministry to troubled Christians, Steve walks where other writers avoid (and consequently leave the reader unchanged). This book is a spotlight on the reality of human decisions and what causes them."

—**Dr. Robert Cornwall**, co-author, *The Five Foundations of Marriage*; pastor to pastors (for 60 years)

DISCERNING
and
DEFEATING
the AHAB
SPIRIT

DISCERNING
and
DEFEATING
the AHAB
SPIRIT

The Key to Breaking Free from Jezebel

STEVE SAMPSON

Chosen

a division of Baker Publishing Group
Grand Rapids, Michigan

Published by Chosen Books
a division of Baker Publishing Group
P.O. Box 6287, Grand Rapids, MI 49516-6287
www.chosenbooks.com

Printed in the United States of America

Library of Congress Cataloging-in-Publication Data
Sampson, Steve, 1948–
    Discerning and defeating the Ahab spirit : the key to breaking free from Jezebel / Steve Sampson.
       p.   cm.
    Includes bibliographical references.
    ISBN 978-0-8007-9494-1 (pbk.)
    1. Assertiveness (Psychology)—Religious aspects—Christianity. 2. Ahab, King of Israel. 3. Jezebel, Queen, consort of Ahab, King of Israel. I. Title.
BV4647.A78S25 2010
241'.4—dc22   2010014605

To protect the privacy of those who have shared their stories with the author, some details and names have been changed.

10   11   12   13   14   15   16   7   6   5   4   3   2   1

Contents

Acknowledgments

Thank You, sweet Holy Spirit, for Your wonderful guidance and wisdom and for ordering my steps as You led me through my own personal process of healing and deliverance. I love You for the way You guide us into Your truth.

My heartfelt appreciation goes to my good friend Melodie Thomas for her invaluable assistance in completing this manuscript. Melodie, the depth of your own personal experiences has contributed greatly in revealing the compassion and glory of God. May He bless you for your willingness to be an overcomer.

Thanks also to Judith Vercher, LMFT, a Certified Relationship Therapist and an anointed counselor. Judith, your profound understanding of human behavior has provided so many insights into understanding the conflicts we all face in life. The Lord bless you for the professional input you provided toward better understanding this topic.

To Ann and Fred Goocher, my sister and brother-in-law—you have been a continual source of encouragement in my life. Thank you for your prayers and the selfless time spent in helping me to draw on the power of the Holy Spirit.

I am especially appreciative of my friend Pastor John Crane for being a voice into my life and seeking God with me. It goes without saying that you have greatly influenced me in my walk with the Lord. The wisdom and the profound insight that the Lord gives you always leaves me amazed.

Lastly, I wish to express my deepest gratitude to all of you who have prayed and stood with me through the unfolding of this manuscript. May God bless you and honor you for your unselfish devotion in seeking Him and lifting up the needs of His people.

Foreword

I was part of the Woodstock generation, one of whose anthems was a song written by Joni Mitchell and performed by Crosby, Stills, Nash and Young commemorating that gathering at Yasgur's Farm near White Lake, New York, in 1969. The gist of the message these troubadours endeavored to get across: "We've got to get ourselves back to the garden." The "garden" meant paradise or Eden. It was the cry of that generation to get back there.

Indeed, none of us lives in such an idyllic place. And as human beings we all have feet of clay. Long before we reach full maturity, most of us have had to face dysfunction again and again, both in ourselves and in others. The percentage of dysfunctional families continues to climb in today's society, and children are increasingly at risk of becoming conditioned by these dysfunctions—only to grow up and repeat, or perhaps exceed, these dysfunctions in their generation. It has been said that what one generation allows in moderation, the next generation will permit in excess.

As a matter of fact, from a scriptural perspective, there is no one who is not dysfunctional. That shatters our egos for sure. To deny that reality, however, is to deny the reality

11

of sin and its effects on our personal lives and on the lives of those with whom we interact. Not only has sin separated humans from their Creator, it has also separated humans from each other.

The sad truth is, none of us in our own ability can ever get back to the Garden. It took the redemptive work of Christ to get the Garden not only to us, but actually in us. When God, the Great Gardener, plants His Word in our hearts, He begins clearing away unwanted vegetation from the soil of our lives that would hinder our growth into the likeness of Christ. He begins to reclaim the garden of our souls for His glory.

This cleanup work requires our cooperation. We have to experience the processes that the prophet Isaiah speaks of: "Let every valley be lifted up, and every mountain and hill be made low; and let the rough ground become a plain, and the rugged terrain a broad valley" (Isaiah 40:4, NASB). There are low places in our internal geography that need to be exalted, high places that need to be brought down and rough places that need to be made smooth, so that the glory of God's image can be seen in us. That does not happen without our working out what God is working in.

One area of dysfunction that leaves people crippled, both personally and generationally, can be seen in the spectrum of behaviors that lie between passivity and aggression. Nothing is more self-defeating than passive behavior and the passive beliefs that lead to it. Nothing is so destructive as aggressive behavior, which always stems from unhealthy beliefs about oneself and others. Between the farthest edges of the scale between passivity and aggression runs a whole range of quite ungodlike behaviors (from which we get the word *ungodly*). These behaviors lead to self-sabotage or to sabotaging others. Both extremes hinder our experience of the abundant life Christ promised and the abundant outcomes (fruits) that go with it.

The root system of passive behavior extends deep into the soil of the human soul and lives below the level of consciousness in a multitude of fears, along with shame and guilt. Passive people are afraid to speak up for themselves. They tend to isolate themselves from others. They value themselves less than they do others. They hurt themselves to avoid hurting others. And the list goes on and on.

On the opposite end of the spectrum, aggressive people strive to control and manipulate every conversation and every situation. They are not good at listening to others or valuing them or their opinions, and they show it by interrupting and talking over people. They are good at intimidation, and they use their body posture, body space and eyes to belittle those who seek to share their perceived space or territory. They are inconsiderate of both the feelings and requests of others. Here as well, their list of dysfunctional behavior goes on and on.

Both of these behavioral dysfunctions contradict an affirming lifestyle of mutually preferring one another in honor and love.

The midpoint between passive and aggressive behavior is assertive behavior. When you decide it is important to respect your humanity and the humanity of others, you begin to love your neighbor as yourself. When you allow the Holy Spirit to develop assertive behaviors in your life, you begin to speak more openly, with a pleasant and appealing tone. You build rapport with others more quickly. You win support for your cause. You participate with others instead of isolating or controlling them. You value yourself as equal to (but not less than or more than) others. And this list goes on and on.

Passivity and aggression are learned behaviors—meaning if you learned them, you can unlearn them and develop new learning in the area of how to behave assertively. My dear friend Steve Sampson has done a thorough and marvelous job of taking you step-by-step through the process of recognizing and unlearning these unhealthy and unaffirming behaviors. He also shows you the way into a life filled with the peace of God that passes all understanding and the joy that is your birthright in Christ. Steve effectively uses the templates of Ahab and Jezebel to personify these extremes in behavior, applying simple truths from Scripture to show you how to live assertively instead, the way Jesus lived.

Take your time reading through each chapter in this book. Consider the real-life examples Steve shares and let the Spirit of God begin to point out those areas in you that pose your greatest challenge toward living assertively. This little tome, if you do what Steve invites you to do, will change your life!

It is time for us to practice a whole new set of behaviors by practicing a whole new set of beliefs based on the truth in Christ. As Steve demonstrates in these pages and in his life, you can discern and defeat the Ahab spirit, and break free from the Jezebel spirit, through the power of the Holy Spirit and your own willingness to follow where He leads. As your mind is renewed, so will your life be renewed.

My thanks to Steve for his transparency and for offering us this pathway to freedom. Happy reading!

Bishop Mark J. Chironna, Ph.D.
The Master's Touch International Church
Mark Chironna Ministries
Orlando, Florida

Introduction

Remember the story of Jezebel? If you do, you will recall that she ended up as the namesake of control freaks everywhere. Jezebels manipulate, intimidate and dominate. In fact, the original Jezebel was so dominant in her relationship with her spouse that she is probably more well-known than her husband, even though he was a king of Israel.

This king, Ahab, is the namesake of those of us who passively tend to relinquish our God-given power and authority. The pain and crippling discomfort of being an Ahab will continue for us until we confront our patterns of relating to others and recognize how we misrepresent ourselves. Only if we take these steps can we seek change and God's balance in our lives. If we do not take these steps, we continue producing the same passive responses to the conflicts we face— complete with feelings of inferiority and unworthiness. We continue avoiding conflict at any cost—even at the cost of not expressing our own identity. We forget that our worth is based on being made in God's image, not on how we please others, and we learn to "roll over and play dead" rather than stand up and risk being who we really are.

Of course, we do not mean to write this script for ourselves. But it is as if we wear a sign around our necks that says, "Feel free to abuse me, walk on me, insult me and usurp my authority." This eventually takes a serious toll on our emotions and continually wears down our self-esteem. We also can be taken in by how well Ahab-Jezebel relationships seem to work—at least outwardly—for a season. Jezebel dictated not only how to act, but how to think. Her husband was a king who lost his identity and power because he refused to stand up. What a risk he took! When Ahab gave away his rightful position and power, he brought terrible repercussions on himself and on the whole kingdom.

The truth is that Ahab-like personalities often attract and are attracted to Jezebels (whatever the cost) because of an unconscious desire to balance themselves. But trying to balance ourselves in such a way is a self-centered, controlling maneuver aimed at gaining power over another person or changing another person to meet an unconscious need within ourselves.

The key word as we confront this problem is *assertiveness*. Most people fall into two categories: Either they tend to have a passive nature (Ahab) or they tend to have a more aggressive nature (Jezebel). As our model and example, however, Jesus was neither passive nor aggressive. Rather, He was assertive. He always dealt with people in an assertive manner, presenting them with their choices, but respecting their right to choose.

Those of us with Ahab-like tendencies need to repent of our passive behaviors and ask the Holy Spirit to reveal the root of this lifestyle and show us how we became trapped in it. Passivity is a spiritual problem. It stems from the fear of man—a self-abasement scenario of not caring enough to embrace our own dignity as redeemed human beings. This comes not from the perfect identity of our human spirit, which is whole and complete in Christ, but from our imperfect soul, which needs to be restored. After years of living in the shadows of passivity, I now know that passive behavior produces suppressed emotions that affect every relationship. Put simply, passive people are simply afraid to be who they are.

Many genuine believers are guilty of living their lives by eating from the wrong tree. Their decisions and responses are from the Tree of Knowledge of Good and Evil, rather than the Tree of Life. To live assertively, the way Jesus did, is to always choose life—to look at every situation from God's perspective (life). To live passively or aggressively means we look at things from our own limited perspective (being the judge between good and evil).

Passive people feel a need to please everyone and will usually give away their power and be slow to speak their minds. They are slow to defend themselves and will accept insults too easily. Aggressive people, on the other hand, tend to be bossy, take power, feel they can talk down to others and indicate that their input and opinions are far more important than anyone else's.

The Ahab spirit (the tendency toward passivity) and the Jezebel spirit (the propensity toward aggression and control) can be overcome as we learn to live assertively, as Jesus did. This involves taking a long, hard look at our responses, or lack of responses, and being brutally honest with ourselves.

A serious Christian will be passionate about increasing the Kingdom of God and being an instrument in God's hand. But if our hearts are passive, we provide little for God to work with. Two things seem to kill our expectation that we will experience the power of God in our lives. First, if we succumb to feelings of unworthiness, we have little faith to give to God. "But without faith it is impossible to please Him" (Hebrews 11:6). Second, if we capitulate to thinking that says, *If it be Thy will*, then we are in a posture of faithlessness, not living in agreement for the manifestations of His promises.

Jesus paid the price for all we need through His sacrifice, giving His life on the cross. He thereby has called us into a covenant with Him. We are joint heirs! (See Romans 8:17.)

In fact, before we ask, God has already said yes. "For all the promises of God in Him are Yes, and in Him Amen, to the glory of God through us" (2 Corinthians 1:20). Personally, I want to live in such a way as to bring glory and increase to the Kingdom of God and do as much damage to the kingdom of darkness as possible. It is hard to live proactively in that way while being passive.

Spiritual maturity is far more than a matter of no longer sinning. Maturity comes when we begin to see life from God's perspective so we can become a blessing to the Kingdom of God. Paul wrote:

> That the God of our Lord Jesus Christ, the Father of glory, may give to you the spirit of wisdom and revelation in the knowledge of Him, the eyes of your understanding being enlightened; that you may know what is the hope of His calling, what are the riches of the glory of His inheritance in the saints.
>
> Ephesians 1:17–18

Maturity comes when we begin to see by the Spirit, and we stop trusting our sense realm. As believers filled with the Holy Spirit, we have a new set of eyes and a new set of ears.

The ultimate expression of spiritual immaturity is an attitude of passivity, along with a refusal to change. God intends to bring change in our lives "till we all come to the unity of the faith . . . to a perfect man, to the measure of the stature of the fullness of Christ" (Ephesians 4:13). God loves us too much to let us stay where we are, and too many of us have let the Ahab spirit keep a chokehold on our destiny. Since God is all about change, we must be willing to change. Something in us must exhibit a willingness to confront every area that the Holy Spirit puts His finger on. Again, this means that we have to be brutally honest with ourselves.

As we deal with passive and aggressive behavior, we quickly recognize that our effectiveness for God is limited by our willingness to cooperate with His Holy Spirit. Being a Christian is not enough; reading the Bible, praying and even regular church attendance are not enough. Even churches can be great places to hide from God! We can look as though we have it together but be living unplugged from God, without a fervent heart. "The backslider *in heart* will be filled with his own ways" (Proverbs 14:14, emphasis added).

As individual believers, we need to come to the realization that we are responsible for our own lives. We can make an assertive decision to walk with God until all our wounds are healed, recognizing that God will show us the truth about ourselves and give us the wisdom to mature. As David said, "Behold, You desire truth in the inward parts, and in the hidden part You will make me to know wisdom" (Psalm 51:6).

As you read this book, I am confident that the Holy Spirit will give you a fresh understanding of how much you are valued. God will help you plug in to the significant purpose He has for your life. Only when you tap into the assertiveness that comes from being in Christ can you truly discover your identity and enjoy the benefits of being a son or daughter of God.

Part 1

An Age-Old Battle

*Pitting the Passivity of Ahab
against the Aggressiveness of Jezebel*

Whether we have a passive nature like Ahab
or a controlling nature like Jezebel, we miss
out on living the life God intended for us. In
order to pursue that life, we need to understand how our passive or aggressive spirits
hinder us.

1

A Passive Spirit

Tears streamed down Eric's cheeks as he once again heard his father's crushing words of disapproval. He was so proud of painting the fence, but he did not clean the brushes properly, and his dad's rebuke pierced his young heart. Eric grew up in a home where his father was a perfectionist and a workaholic. Never once did he hear his father say, "You did a good job" or "I'm proud of you" or "Let's do something special together." From as far back as he could remember, Eric's perception was that his father measured him only by the amount of work he accomplished. Instead of hearing the statements of approval he craved, Eric only heard his dad say, "You forgot to finish this" or "Now I've got another job for you."

It seemed impossible for Eric to please his father. (By the way, the names and personal details in these stories have been changed to protect the individuals involved.) Eric grieved over this and began blaming himself, feeling that he was a failure, a loser, never able to do anything right. Sometimes he would stand in front of the mirror and feel such self-loathing that he would call himself hateful names. As a teenager, Eric struggled with feelings of isolation, never feeling as though he was part of any group. Instead of trying out for athletic teams, he would convince himself that he was not good enough. He feared rejection so much that he rarely socialized or asked girls out on dates.

Eric was too young to recognize that these patterns were not entirely his problem, but stemmed from his father's spiritual, emotional and mental issues. His father was of the opinion that a person's worth is totally based on his or her performance—if you are not producing, you are worthless. He could not even relate to children until they were old enough to work.

As Eric grew older, he lived in the prison of trying to perform for and please his dad, looking for acceptance anywhere he could. This neediness would overwhelm him as he continued to seek the approval, attention and validation he still desperately desired from his father. This caused so much turmoil within him that it brought about depression, resentment, feelings of worthlessness, self-hatred, withdrawal and an inability to control his behavior. Out of all this Eric became very passive, unable to feel good enough about himself to take any initiative in setting goals, making healthy decisions and living a fulfilled life.

Eric was in great bondage to his father's pattern of performance-based living. His dad's critical remarks were like video clips inside his mind. Even after he left home, went to college, married and started a family, these video clips continued to play: "Eric, you're a failure." By then it was no longer about his father—Eric was trapped in the past. Passivity ruled his life.

As an adult, Eric lived as a victim. Early in his marriage, he could not function with positive, assertive behavior, and his lack of confidence caused him to defer to his wife on major decisions instead of showing strong, positive leadership. This affected his marriage as his wife struggled to respect him. When children came along, he saw them as his little friends rather than as children who needed his guidance and mentoring. He would leave the disciplining of the children up to his wife, who would often tell him she needed him to step up to the plate and share the responsibilities.

However, Eric felt so inadequate in these roles that he would emotionally "check out." Instead of hearing his wife and communicating proactively and assertively, he chose to escape through various mindless activities. He would spend hours in front of the television or computer screen. He would go through times of escaping reality by sleeping for long periods. He was notorious for starting project after project but never following through to the finish. His whole life was falling apart because none of these issues was ever resolved. His work also suffered because he just could not stop feeling like a failure.

Finally, Eric began to battle bouts of depression and felt powerless to change any part of his life. In a vicious cycle of trying to please everyone and ultimately pleasing no one, Eric felt he had nowhere to go and no place to turn. Eric had become a modern-day Ahab. Just as Ahab became a man who gave away his power—even though he was the king of Israel—so Eric had succumbed to a life without victory, overcome with depression and hopelessness.

Years later, after finally confronting his patterns of passivity with the help of counselors, Eric was able to recognize that the problem was not entirely his—rather, his father's unhealthy perfectionism had propelled him into a spiral of defeat. Eric started to break free of these old patterns and began to feel a sense of self-worth. He stopped carrying shame and began to get in touch with who he really was— by his heavenly Father's definition. At last Eric was no longer his father's victim, but his own man.

Living in Passivity

While I am not Eric, I can certainly relate to what it is like to be passive. One fall afternoon I was visiting a friend's home, enjoying fellowship with a group of people. I was conversing with Richard, a doctor, with whom I had been friends for several years. We had been enjoying casual conversation and having a delightful time. But that quickly came to a stop when at one point Richard and I looked out the window and watched a man with a slight limp walk down the street. The doctor commented that he could tell that the man had a problem with a certain vertebra just by the way he walked. I joked, "Or maybe he has hemorrhoids."

The doctor's wife, however, mocked and insulted me in front of everyone and said that because I was not a doctor, I should keep my mouth shut. Her harsh comment was extremely painful and caught me by surprise. I am not sure why she felt the need to make such a statement. I am not always quick with a response, especially when I am caught off guard. So rather than defend myself, I just hung my head. Today, I am still disappointed at myself for not defending my statement as a joke and for not telling her to stop talking to me in such a rude manner. I realize now that a healthier, more assertive response would have been to tell her that she was wrong to misinterpret my lighthearted statement so quickly and tell her that I deserved an apology.

Since then I have learned (and honestly, am still learning) that this kind of pain never goes away until we recognize our unhealthy patterns of relating to others. We need to realize how we misrepresent ourselves. Only then can we seek change and God's balance in our lives. If we do not take these steps, we increasingly produce the same passive responses to conflict—complete with feelings of inferiority and unworthiness. We continue in patterns of living that avoid relational conflict and sidestep expressing ourselves at any cost. We do not like ourselves, sometimes to the point of loathing.

What's the Problem?

Maybe you have been living like this—avoiding relational conflict at all costs. Maybe your actions say to others, "Abuse me, walk on me, insult me and usurp my authority." That is quite a message, and you have never really identified why you are sending it out. The problem is being stuck in a pattern of passivity.

Just what is passivity? Is it a demonic influence? Is it a personality trait? Is it laziness or spiritual weakness clothed in a fear of asserting yourself?

Passivity can be all of the above. It has its roots in demonic blindness, where Satan assaults people's self-worth to the point that it suffocates their ability to stand up for themselves and confront situations and conflicts. This blindness paralyzes individuals to the extent that they choose not to say or do anything.

Passivity can also be an inherited personality trait that comes from seeing passivity modeled by parents and other significant people in our lives. I will explain more about this later when I talk about how my passive mother "taught" me passivity.

Sometimes passivity can result from confusion. Even people in ministry may confuse subservience with submissiveness and must be careful to give proper counsel. Subservient behavior is passive behavior—and it is wrong. Submissive behavior is being supportive, agreeable and willing—all good things— whereas subservient behavior is passively giving up one's rights. For example, if a husband asks his wife to sin against God, should she be "submissive" and agree? Of course not! We must be careful not to confuse that kind of subservience with true submissiveness.

Most importantly, I believe that passivity is a spiritual problem. It stems from the fear of man; a self-abasement scenario of not caring enough to embrace our own dignity as redeemed human beings. Again, this comes not from our redeemed human spirit, but rather from our soul that is in need of restoration—our mind, will and emotions.

What I describe here is the personality of King Ahab. We find his story in the Old Testament book of 1 Kings. He was the husband of Queen Jezebel. By the way, Queen Jezebel's spirit or attitude also operates freely in our society today. And it can be labeled as demonic because people who experience extreme wounds or deep insecurity succumb to the spiritual blindness of demonic forces. It also can be hereditary or environmental (learned behaviors), usually traced back to the modeling someone received as a child, or from a child so undisciplined that he always got his own way and now functions as a spoiled child in an adult body. These aggressive individuals manipulate, intimidate and dominate to accomplish their own wills and agendas and have no respect for the person who allows them such control. And these personalities know no gender—both men and women can be passive or aggressive, Jezebel or Ahab.

Ahab's Passivity

As you might expect with the passive personality that Ahab exhibited, Jezebel had much more notoriety because of how wicked and evil she was. She killed the prophets of the Lord and carried out her agenda to destroy anyone in her path. Of course, Ahab's passive personality did not mean he was a nice guy. The author of 1 Kings wrote, "Ahab did more to provoke the LORD God of Israel to anger than all the kings of Israel who were before him," and, "There was no one like Ahab who sold himself to do wickedness in the sight of the LORD, because Jezebel his wife stirred him up" (1 Kings 16:33; 21:25).

Ahab married Jezebel, who was an idol worshiper, in disobedience to the Israelites' covenant with God. But Ahab perpetuated his disobedience by never standing up to Jezebel. Instead, he abdicated to her his God-given authority as king (and husband).

In 1 Kings 21, Scripture provides a classic example of Ahab's passivity. It relates that on one occasion, he desired a vineyard adjacent to his palace. It was owned by Naboth, so Ahab approached him and said, "Give me your vineyard, that I may have it for a vegetable garden, because it is near, next to my house; and for it I will give you a vineyard better than it. Or, if it seems good to you, I will give you its worth in money" (verse 2). But Naboth would not negotiate with Ahab, saying, "The LORD forbid that I should give the inheritance of my fathers to you!" (verse 3).

In response to Naboth's refusal, Ahab began to pout—a classic symptom of passivity. "So Ahab went into his house sullen and displeased because of the word which Naboth the Jezreelite had spoken to him. . . . And he lay down on his bed, and turned away his face, and would eat no food" (verse 4).

Think about that! Here was a grown man—a king—pouting like a toddler who did not get a cookie before dinner. In my *Webster's* dictionary, *pouting* is literally defined as "to thrust out the lips, as in sullenness or displeasure." It is an "inward expression of silent resentment or protest" that someone resorts to rather than facing conflict or disagreement. Pouting says to all who see it, "I'm afraid to stand up for myself." Adults who pout eventually experience feelings of self-loathing and incompleteness.

When Ahab "lay down on his bed, and turned away his face, and would eat no food," he displayed another classic symptom of passivity. In modern terms, we call his actions depression. Depression is usually rooted in self-centeredness and anger turned in on oneself. Rather than face the challenges of life outwardly, Ahab went to sleep. Sleep can be the passive individual's way of escaping truth and responsibility. Because of his inward turmoil and pain, Ahab did not want to talk to anyone and could not eat.

Ahab's passivity opened the door for the aggressive and controlling Jezebel to take over! First she scolded Ahab: "Why is your spirit so sullen that you eat no food?" (verse 5). Then she demeaned Ahab's authority and manhood by saying, "You now exercise authority over Israel! Arise, eat food, and let your heart be cheerful; I will give you the vineyard of Naboth the Jezreelite" (verse 7).

Control freaks (Jezebels) always take power and authority that do not belong to them. And passive personalities (Ahabs) always let them get away with it, or Ahabs give their power up, not realizing how controlling they are themselves. Yes, Ahabs can be just as selfish, controlling and even manipulative because they give their power away in order to get love in return. Ahab himself did things for Jezebel in order to get what he wanted.

While Ahab continued his pouting, the manipulative Jezebel moved craftily. She wrote letters in Ahab's name, sealed them with his seal and sent them to the city's leaders. She hired two scoundrels to bear false witness against Naboth in front of the people, telling them to say that Naboth "blasphemed God and the king" (verse 10). Her scheme succeeded. She incited the people to anger, and they took Naboth outside the city and stoned him to death.

Returning to Ahab, Jezebel said, "Arise, take possession of the vineyard of Naboth the Jezreelite, which he refused to give you for money; for Naboth is not alive, but dead" (verse 15). Ahab dutifully accepted his wife's reprehensible deed—content that he got the land that he wanted and not caring that it resulted in Naboth's death.

The bottom line is that passively giving away your authority qualifies as an evil deed. Look at the result when Ahab did so. Abdicating your God-given authority is just as sinful an act as its opposite, aggressively usurping the authority of others.

Are You Trapped in Passivity?

Years later, I still feel frustrated when I remember incidents in which I was insulted and demeaned but did not assert myself.

Many people would not even remember these events, but my passive nature causes me to remember the hurts as if they just happened yesterday. I now recognize that we passive people suppress emotions, which affects all our relationships. We are afraid to be who we are.

Those of us who have walked around with such bottled-up feelings know that they do not just disappear. These emotions eventually turn into depression and anxiety, as well as passive-aggressive behaviors such as rage. As a result, we passively seek to manipulate others with the rage we feel inside. We might even outwardly displace this anger onto others, especially those who love us. Passive behavior ultimately becomes passive-aggressive, and the mindset of a passive-aggressive person is, "I don't get mad. I get even."

Satan tries to get his hooks into our lives early, especially into those of us who were never validated or taught we had value. When children experience emotional pain or traumatic events without the intervention of an adult ally, they are too young and immature to process what is truth and what is a lie. Most times they will internalize what they have experienced and believe the lies that their caretakers have modeled and the devil has reinforced. In a healthy scenario, with an adult present to help them process difficult events, children can better understand how to cope and get back to the job of being children instead of taking on adult issues. The problem is, many of us who did not have the advantage of an adult ally to help us through things grow up without correcting our unhealthy responses and behaviors. Then by our example, we teach our children the same unhealthy coping patterns we used.

The devil is a liar and a deceiver and takes advantage of anyone he can. Although he was defeated at the cross of Calvary, he goes about like a roaring lion, seeking to devour anyone who will listen to his lies (see 1 Peter 5:8–9). Jesus said the devil comes to steal, kill and destroy (see John 10:10). If a child does not experience validation and encouragement, a door opens to the enemy to plant seeds of rejection and unworthiness that can affect a person's choices for a lifetime. But we have a better option than believing the lies. James 4:7 tells us, "Resist the devil and he will flee from you." Once a person begins to have knowledge of God, he or she must also recognize and challenge demonic forces and demonic thinking. "And do not be conformed to this world, but be transformed by the renewing of your mind" (Romans 12:2).

Although the devil is a defeated foe, many succumb to lies that have entered through an open door of wrong thinking. Many of us are deceived into believing that we are victims who are powerless to change the things that are not working in our lives. However, the Bible clearly says that we *can* cast down these strongholds that have been erected in our lives and minds: "[Cast] down imaginations, and every high thing that exalteth itself against the knowledge of God" (2 Corinthians 10:5, KJV). The good news is that as believers, we have authority over the enemy, and he has no right to depress, oppress or possess a child of God.

In order to effectively break the spirit of passivity and wield our God-given authority to change things, we must first understand the difference between passive and aggressive personalities. The next chapter details what each of these character traits looks like.

2

Passive versus Aggressive

Everyone who knew David considered him a nice guy. He seemed to make no enemies and meet no strangers. However, when he took a job at a marketing company, things began to change. At first, he told his friends how much he loved his new job, but within a few months he was at his wits' end. His immediate supervisor, Joe, assigned difficult jobs to David that no one else was willing to accept. At first, he took this in stride, but soon the stress and workload became too much for him to handle. To make matters worse, his boss never gave him credit. Instead, the man took credit himself for work David had done. This boss even received a promotion for projects he had not done.

Because David had a passive nature, he continued pretending things were fine, until one day he collapsed at work and was rushed to the emergency room. Thankfully, he was diagnosed only with exhaustion, and he quickly recovered. This episode ended up as a blessing in disguise because through it David had to learn to draw boundaries. His supervisor denied everything, so David approached the owners of the company and explained his work situation. Soon he was reassigned to a different department and began to enjoy success.

Like David, those of us who are passive often do not recognize our own passivity until we are forced to do so. The same holds true of those who are aggressive. However, we can learn a lot about what it means to be passive or aggressive by contrasting passive and aggressive character traits:

- *Overmerciful versus overlegalistic.* Passive people like Ahab tend to be overmerciful, seeing the best in every person and overlooking too much. They forgive others too quickly (not making them aware of their offense) and also forgive people who have not asked for forgiveness and are not even remorseful. This almost certainly guarantees the abuser's continued behavior. Aggressive people like Jezebel are on the other extreme—harsh in their expectations and unforgiving when people do not meet their unrealistic expectations.

- *Walking away from a person versus walking over a person.* People with passive Ahab personalities quickly give away their power and walk away in order to avoid conflict. They find it easier to push their feelings inside. On the other hand, people with aggressive personalities seem to have no concern or conscience about whom they step on and use, as long as they get their way.

- *Avoiding confrontation versus in-your-face confrontation.* Passive people avoid confrontation at all costs and will even blame themselves when others insult or betray them. However, aggressive people have no problem handing out insults and pushing blame on whomever they happen to choose. They have no regard for others' feelings, and will more or less tell you this.

- *Peacekeepers versus peacemakers.* Passive personalities are notorious for being peacekeepers. They want the temporary, immediate gratification of keeping the peace

at any price rather than "making peace" by boldly dealing with the issues at hand, which would result in more
permanent, long-term gratification.

- *Grumbling under one's breath versus open verbal abuse.*
  People with passive personalities will resent verbal assaults, but they will refuse to take the offender to task
  and stop the behavior. Instead, they usually walk away
  grumbling. Aggressive people feel free to openly vent,
  abuse others and tell them off. Just minutes later, they
  will act as if nothing happened, even though they have
  left resentful people with wounded hearts in their wake.
  Jezebel personalities are so self-centered that they do
  not even realize they have severely damaged the people
  who happened to be in their destructive path, and Ahab
  personalities leave others feeling responsible for them
  as victims.

- *Do not mind being wrong (if you'll approve of me)
  versus refusing ever to be wrong (I'll love you if you see
  things my way).* Passive people often have such a need
  for approval that they will take the blame for anything
  if they perceive it as winning them your acceptance.
  Aggressive people will love you until you disagree with
  them! Then that love becomes a destructive hatred for
  you, and they will even go to the point of trying to
  destroy you and your reputation.

- *Fear of nonacceptance versus fear of rejection.* While
  passive people will do almost anything to gain acceptance, aggressive people (who are always insecure and
  often wounded people) have a huge fear of rejection.
  Their actions come out of an "attack mode" because
  they are determined never to experience rejection
  again.

- *Low self-esteem (clothed in nice) versus low self-esteem
  (clothed in fear of more hurt).* Passive people are usually
  nice people—too nice. They have low self-worth and

35

try to gain ground by winning acceptance. Aggressive people also have low self-esteem, but usually they are bold, arrogant and pushy—all in an effort (because of old wounds) to avoid more hurt.

- *Fear of what people think of me versus fear of people not agreeing with me.* The fear of man totally binds most passive people. They spend amazing amounts of energy trying to please everyone—even those they do not know or those who could not care less about them. Aggressive individuals, on the other hand, are so insecure that they see anyone who chooses to disagree with them as the enemy. Filled with their own insecurities, aggressive people perceive any type of correction as more rejection.

- *Anger directed inward versus anger directed toward others.* Passive people are notorious for directing anger and insults back at themselves. If something goes wrong, they simply blame themselves. They often have major anger issues and will ultimately become passive-aggressive. Aggressive people pour their anger out on anyone who is available. They rarely look at themselves because they are so convinced they are right. These aggressive personalities are self-appointed figures who think one of their roles is to correct the rest of the world. Sometimes they are sarcastically referred to as "gods in training."

- *Accepting blame too easily versus projecting blame (you made me do it).* Typically, passive people will quickly embrace blame in a situation in order to put everyone else at ease. While this is actually a kind of a false humility, passive people have the goal of making everyone happy again in order to increase their own self-worth. Like Jezebel, aggressive people will take blame for nothing! Even when caught in a wrong, their defense is, "You made me do it." "Yes, I robbed the bank, but it's your fault because you didn't give me enough money . . ."

Destructive Results

From this simple list, we can see how destructive both passive and aggressive behaviors can be. For example, I have encountered many men who gave up their authority long ago. They now live in passivity, exerting no leadership in their homes. Some can tell you the very day they abdicated their authority, choosing not to deal with a conflict or set boundaries with a controlling wife.

At the same time, I have met many women who have given up their power and strength in dealing with a controlling husband. Rather than feeling empowerment and a God-given worth, they have capitulated to a lifestyle of passivity and visionless regret. They are satisfied with survival and often feel trapped in the dynamics of their relationship because of fear, rather than standing up for their rightful place. Simply put, in many marriage relationships the woman sells out for security and the man sells out for sex. The bottom line: Neither is happy nor fulfilled, and they will never experience true intimacy.

In all these cases, the passive individuals have chosen to live a lie and pay the price of not confronting the aggressive people in their lives. Defeated and deflated, they accept this empty life with no outward protest. How sad, when Jesus promised us abundant life—life to the full.

A Desire to Please God

If passive Ahab behaviors and aggressive Jezebel behaviors are both so destructive, what kind of life should we pursue instead?

Most of us are familiar with at least parts of the story of David from the Old Testament. God eventually raised up David to take Saul's place as Israel's king. David was not a passive person by nature. The psalms he authored show us that David desired to pursue the Lord in all that he said and did. Because of this, Samuel described David as "a man after His [God's] own heart" (1 Samuel 13:14).

I find it interesting that the Bible does not say David had a great doctrinal or belief system, or that he possessed eloquent preaching skills. Scripture even clearly shows that David did not lead a sin-free life. However, pleasing God and living out the will of God were at the forefront in David's heart. His life was effective when he contemplated God's purposes for his life. Put most simply, overall David lived a God-centered, not self-centered, existence.

This is not true of passive people. We go through life aiming for self-preservation and not drawing attention to ourselves. We rarely take the initiative, we are not self-starters, and usually we are waiting for someone else to "discover" us or seek us out. Then we are disappointed or even angry if others ignore our position or do not acknowledge us. It is hard to focus on God and live out His will for us when we are trapped by passivity and all its negative effects.

Later in David's life, he did lose his focus on God, and he sinned as a direct result of passivity. The Bible tells us that one time when David should have been out at battle like other kings, instead he relinquished his authority to others and stayed home in his palace. The rest of this story is well-known: When he should have been leading the armies of Israel, David committed adultery with Bathsheba and then murdered her husband. (See 2 Samuel 11.)

What *is* remarkable is that David soon recognized his sin was against God. In humility, he took responsibility for his actions. As he prayed, he acknowledged, "Against You, You only, have I sinned, and done this evil in Your sight" (Psalm 51:4). While David could have made the case that Bathsheba should not have been in such an easily accessible viewing place, thereby tempting him, he did not blame her. David understood that his failure was his and his alone, and that his sin was against God and God alone.

Even in his failures, David had a heart that reverenced the Lord over his own well-being. This heartfelt reverence carried itself into all aspects of his relationship with God. Like many of us, he had his moments where he succumbed to passive (or aggressive) behaviors that got him into trouble, but he humbly repented and asked for God's forgiveness and help. In essence, David willingly surrendered his own will to pursue God's will and purpose for his life. David was secure in who he was because he realized that his worth and identity came from God alone.

In the next chapter, let's look at some other examples of passivity, both from the Bible and from modern life, and see just how destructive it can be to us and to our relationships.

3

Self-Defeat, Rebellion and Rejection

My close friend Paul was going through a crisis in his marriage. His wise pastor gave him excellent counsel in dealing with his wife, Cindy, who always showed disdain and disrespect for her husband. Among their friends, Cindy was notorious for usurping Paul's authority. For many years, throughout most of their married life, Paul had lived passively and tried to please Cindy.

Paul's pastor advised him very specifically about how he should approach Cindy. However, each time the pastor tried to instruct him, Paul would interrupt with what he feared Cindy's reaction might be. The fear of his wife's reaction had Paul calculating her responses, which left him totally paralyzed. The pastor would sympathetically laugh, saying, "She has you so controlled that you can't even function because you already know her reaction." Ironically, Cindy did not even have to be present to keep Paul under her control.

Here the wife had the aggressive personality, but in my experience, control does not necessarily have a specific gender. I know of many situations in which a dominating husband verbally and physically abuses his wife, leaving her intimidated. To avoid this, Scripture tells men to deal with their wives as the weaker vessel:

> Husbands, likewise, dwell with them with understanding, giving honor to the wife, as to the weaker vessel, and as being heirs together of the grace of life, that your prayers may not be hindered.
>
> 1 Peter 3:7

To Paul, however, nothing seemed weak about Cindy. He would never have abused her, but he was so bound with passivity that he did not dare to speak assertively to her. He believed he would experience total defeat if he did. Her pattern of intimidation and his reaction to it had stolen his dignity as a human being. Sadly, Paul had given away his authority to his wife long ago. Getting it back required him to get to the root of his behavior, which meant repenting of vows and judgments he had made about his passive mother. He had observed his mother's passivity in action when he was young. She was anything but bold and assertive, and he had adopted her passivity. Then he had lived it out in his marriage, passively trying to please Cindy.

Vows and judgments come back to haunt us if we do not repent of them. Whether we make them as a spoken declaration or simply say them in our hearts, they result in long-term damage. For one thing, they often cause us to react to things too passively or too aggressively. That is one reason Scripture tells us, "Judge not, that you be not judged. For with what judgment you judge, you will be judged; and with the measure you use, it will be measured back to you" (Matthew 7:1–2).

Paul had to learn to be bold and assertive in situations where his typical reaction would have been passivity—not easy to accomplish since he spent his whole childhood watching his mother capitulate to keep the peace. For Paul, change required reprogramming his lifelong thinking and behavior patterns. I have spoken to many passive people like Paul who could pinpoint for me the exact time in their life when they gave their authority away to their spouses. It seemed easier at the time for them to ignore conflict than to deal with it—but that, of course, meant capitulating to passivity.

Jesus told us that the truth will make us free (see John 8:32). But freedom is taken, not given—we have to assert ourselves by standing up for our convictions and not expect that freedom will happen automatically. Sometimes people feel as if they need to be given permission to have their own point of view. Fear will keep us from stating or acting on the truth. In this case, it appeared that Cindy had Paul in bondage, and he allowed her to keep him in bondage. Her independence and intimidation embodied the spirit of Jezebel, and Paul's fear of conflict with Cindy was more real to him than the fear of God.

When Paul began to confront his wife's behavior, she went into a rage and threatened him with all manner of consequences. But Paul increasingly realized that the destructive consequences of his passive, Ahab-like behavior were worse for both of them. In fact, right after he first stood up to Cindy, Paul called out to God for more understanding. That very night, he had a dream from the Lord. In the dream, his testicles had been cut off. He woke up crying and asking for a doctor to sew them back on. He knew God was speaking to him, confirming that Cindy's aggressive behavior had emasculated his authority. He also realized that he was asking God to do something he had to do himself—take back his authority, of course with God's help.

As Paul continued to stand his ground with Cindy, he not only gained back his self-respect, but he also gained the respect of his children. They began to see the change and rejoiced with him. If Paul had not stood up to Cindy, he easily could have lost their respect forever. Worse, they, too, might have embodied Ahab-like characteristics in their own lives and become the victims of a Jezebel in their relationships.

King Ahab's passive behavior actually cost him all his children. Israel's King Jehu showed no compassion for Ahab or his descendants and had all of them killed: "So Jehu killed all who remained of the house of Ahab in Jezreel, and all his great men and his close acquaintances and his priests, until he left him none remaining" (2 Kings 10:11). It is tragic when we do not deal with our passive behavior, instead passing it down to our children by our example. However, we can be the ones that confront that behavior and cut it off forever—giving glory to God.

Although Cindy was reluctant, Paul pursued change. He took back his power and drew a line, saying to her in so many words, "I do love you, but you're not going to talk to me or treat me in a controlling way anymore." As he faced this issue, Paul began to grow exponentially in his relationship with the Lord. His long-lost joy returned, and he began to feel like a worthwhile human being again. Fear, intertwined with passivity, could not bind him any longer.

Sadly, Cindy did not appreciate Paul's new assertiveness and sued him for divorce. Although they spent a lot of time in marriage counseling, Cindy's anger grew even greater as time went on. She wanted no part of the changes in Paul, knowing she could no longer control him. Paul was greatly disappointed, but he knew he had no choice but to move on with his life. However, he was also happy that he felt like a man again, and he was confident that God had great plans for his life.

Maybe you have responded with a fear of conflict in a similar situation. You know what you need to do to confront a Jezebel in your life, but before you say a single word or take a single action, you are already thinking to yourself, *If I say this, he or she will respond in this way . . .*

Think closely about that. Because of your passivity, this person already has you under control before a dialogue even begins. It is time to be assertive and respect yourself. Be bold! No more walking on eggshells! You are free to be you, but you have to accept that freedom and act on it. You are a child of God.

What Makes Us Passive?

We explored some of the characteristics of passivity in chapter 2. But let's dig a little deeper and examine how some of us end up possessing these traits.

It is important to note that passive people are not evil people. However, they become allies of evil by not resisting or pushing against the active force of evil. In fact, the word *passive* means "nonacting" or "nonresisting." It actually comes from a Latin word meaning "to suffer." Certainly, some type of suffering is almost always the end result of passivity.

Passive people have become that way by giving up their identities. They will do almost anything to avoid displeasure or disapproval. They also feel an intense need for approval, acceptance and appreciation. The bottom line is that they desperately want to be liked, and they literally (although usually subconsciously) will give up part or all of their identity and individuality just to make sure people will like them.

When withdrawal becomes a comfortable habit for someone, passivity is the result. Passive people usually withdraw from conflict by walking away, leaving the room or taking on a time-consuming project. Some passive people allow verbal or physical abuse without objection or protest. They forgive other people's offenses too quickly and do not confront their offenders assertively. Sometimes they even escape unpleasantness by turning to drugs, alcohol or other types of addictions.

People who find it easiest to live "on the surface" often become passive. Most passive people are extremely slow to communicate their feelings. This will cause almost any relationship to suffer and eventually collapse. Passive people also tend to withhold information—usually because they do not feel their feedback will be acknowledged as noteworthy.

Even behaviors that might seem insignificant can feed passivity and be part of how passive people get through life. For example, some may drop hints instead of directly expressing what they want. Others may pretend to understand even when they do not, instead of simply admitting, "I'm not sure what you're talking about." Others will pretend to remember someone's name rather than simply asking, "What's your name again?"

All of these passive behaviors are rooted in the need to avoid conflict or discomfort in relationships. Once people get into the habit—actually the bondage—of such behaviors, it is amazing how they can go through their entire lives and never break away from this spirit of passivity. They go into eternity with many issues and conflicts unresolved.

Passivity Began with Adam

In the familiar account of humanity's fall, we see Adam playing the role of a victim. He blamed both Eve and God rather than admitting his own guilt (see Genesis 3). Perhaps this victim role lies at the root of all sin—our pride gets in the way and we refuse to take responsibility for our actions. In the next chapter, we will look more closely at how this victim mentality feeds our passivity.

Adam acted passively when he avoided standing up to his wife as she enticed him to disobey God and eat the forbidden fruit. He ate with her in direct disobedience to God's command. Then he responded with passive irresponsibility when confronted by a loving God who asked, "Have you eaten from the tree of which I commanded you that you should not eat?" (Genesis 3:11). Adam's response was drenched with accusation toward God, as Adam declared himself the victim: "The woman whom You gave to be with me, she gave me of the tree, and I ate" (verse 12). In effect, Adam told God, "You're a bad God, and You gave me a bad woman."

Passive behavior never wants to deal responsibly with the issue at hand and loves to become the victim. Of course, this is the easy way out—the path of least resistance. Like Adam, passive people declare, "It's not my fault. Somebody else did this to me." Most would rather even blame God than take responsibility for their own actions.

Not much has changed since Adam's response in the Garden. I am amazed at how many people (including me) blame God for their problems. Many of us say, "God, why did You let this happen?" or "You could have prevented this—why didn't You?" And how many times have we said, "God, You don't really love me or care about me"?

As I dealt with the spirit of passivity in my own life, I eventually came to a turning point where I had to deal with a lot of self-hatred and self-rejection. I took a long look back into my childhood and saw that I was not affirmed enough as a child. At least that is what I perceived as a little boy, even if it was not my parents' intention for me to feel that way. Later, as an adult, I realized that I did not accept and love that little boy either. I hated who he was, just as I perceived that others hated him. I had to assertively accept that little boy of my childhood and let him know, so to speak, that he was affirmed and loved by God. I did that by seeing myself as God sees me and accepting myself the way He made me. I could no longer be the victim. It was time to take back my life!

Saul's Passive Rebellion

When the people of ancient Israel pleaded with God to give them a king so they could be like the nations around them, God gave them a king. However, through the prophet Samuel, God warned them that their king would bring them into terrible bondage (see 1 Samuel 8).

Israel's first king, Saul, was a classic example of passivity and partial obedience. In short, he did what made him feel good rather than what God commanded. Interestingly, it did not take long before Saul's true character was revealed. With his very first edict as king, Saul failed. Out of his passive nature, he ignored the instructions of the Lord regarding the Amalekites. Saul acted with casual disregard and did not fully obey God. Instead of completely destroying the enemy, as God commanded, Saul kept the best cattle and sheep and allowed the opposing king to live. Yet when Samuel approached, Saul boldly declared, "I have performed the commandment of the LORD" (1 Samuel 15:13).

Of course, Samuel confronted Saul in his lie, saying, "What then is this bleating of the sheep in my ears, and the lowing of the oxen which I hear?" (verse 14).

Saul tried to justify his actions and blame others for his disobedience, saying, "But I have obeyed the voice of the LORD, and gone on the mission on which the LORD sent me, and brought back Agag king of Amalek; I have utterly destroyed the Amalekites. But the people took of the plunder, sheep and oxen, the best of the things which should have been utterly destroyed, to sacrifice to the LORD your God in Gilgal" (verses 20–21). Note that Saul blamed the people for his actions—he took no personal responsibility.

Unimpressed, Samuel declared to Saul, "For rebellion is as the sin of witchcraft, and stubbornness is as iniquity and idolatry. Because you have rejected the word of the LORD, He also has rejected you from being king" (verse 23).

If you have a propensity toward passivity, you might find yourself not following God fully and then blaming others for your disobedience. Think about that. Do you take the easy way out in situations rather than being brutally honest with yourself and God? Perhaps you only follow your convictions up to the point of feeling comfortable and trap yourself in partial obedience. For example, maybe God has directed you to spend more time with Him in prayer, or spend more time with your spouse or be more consistent in disciplining your children. But bound with passivity, you only partially obey on these issues. It is the easier way. It is more comfortable. Or perhaps God has spoken to you about confronting a person who has stepped over the line in your relationship. Yet you take the easy way out and tell yourself, *It will work out, and maybe they didn't mean it. Or maybe I'm oversensitive.*

Fear of Rejection

The greatest need of every human being is to be loved. But our greatest fear is rejection. Because passive people fear rejection, they will go to great lengths to avoid confrontation. Or they only deal with issues little by little and just put out the current fires. I use the old cliché "Cutting off the dog's tail an inch at a time" to describe this behavior. I have seen pastors and business leaders who fear confrontation so much that this character trait becomes their demise.

We all want people to accept us and think well of us. But the passive personality—bound by the fear of what people will think or say—continually forgoes opportunities to take a stand. It becomes easier to avoid speaking up when we have been insulted. At the time it seems less painful to bury our true feelings and act as if nothing is wrong when someone violates the boundaries of good behavior. When passive people do confront someone who treated them unpleasantly, they usually soften their statements by saying something like, "I'm sure you didn't mean it that way." But this is also a passive cop-out because it lacks authority and assertiveness.

As Christians, we do not have an option when it comes to forgiving others. We forgive as we have been forgiven. "But if you do not forgive, neither will your Father in heaven forgive your trespasses" (Mark 11:26). But too often, passive people will not hold others accountable for the consequences of their offensive actions. It becomes too easy to sweep things under the rug instead of saying something like, "I forgive you, but I won't be able to loan you money in the future," or "Your outburst caused me a lot of hurt, and I won't allow you to put me in that situation again."

In my own experience, I struggled most in situations where I was offended and verbally abused. I would actually go to the person who offended or hurt me and apologize! I rationalized that I was taking the high road, but really, I was denying my true convictions. Worse, the aggressive person would not accept my apology. I was naïve enough to expect at least an "I'm sorry, too." Instead, I would get a response such as, "You should be sorry" or "Okay, just don't let it happen again."

I also learned that Jezebels (control freaks) never truly forgive you; they save your "offense" as ammunition for future conflicts. The next time a problem arises, every past issue or offense will be brought up in your face. And you were naïve enough to believe it was forgiven and forgotten!

The aggressive, Jezebel-like person also fears rejection. However, these wounded people handle their fears in a much different way than passive, Ahab-like personalities. They are determined never to be hurt again. In the worst sense, their demeanor is, "I'm going to attack you before you attack me." They are usually defensive, cutting and unforgiving. They act as if your opinion or input is worthless, and they believe theirs is right and even in alignment with God's truth. An inflated ego masks their low self-esteem.

The deep-seated fear of rejection is always at work in both passive and aggressive personalities. It can come about from either orphan or victim mentalities, which we will look at next.

4

Orphans and Victims

Larry grew up in a highly dysfunctional home with a very abusive father. When he was around nine years old, his dad frequently beat him and his siblings. One particular day, his dad was beating his eight-year-old sister. Larry, only a year older, finally jumped in between them. His dad knocked him down over and over, and he just got up again and again. He tried to stand against the evil rage of his father and kept declaring, "You can't hurt me." Then his mother tried to intervene, and his dad began to beat her. Their dysfunction seemed to erupt in an endless cycle of abuse, and Larry's grandparents later commented that his parents never should have had kids.

Larry told me he had always loved God, and as a little boy he had asked God to stop the beatings. However, when his prayer was not immediately answered, he felt that God did not care. Reasoning as a young child in the midst of such emotional trauma, Larry determined in his heart that since God did not stop the abuse and pain, He must not care about him, so he was alone and abandoned.

Actually, God did answer his prayer by opening the door for Larry and his siblings to live with his grandparents nearly a year later. But Larry was too young to understand and was already so damaged that he could not perceive that God had indeed heard him and had intervened. It was not until years later, when Larry was in his fifties, that everything changed. One day the Lord spoke to him, *You love Me and you love people, but you don't allow Me or other people to love you.*

Larry knew this was because he did not feel accepted. Later a minister came by their house to pray with Larry and his wife, Kathy. After the pastor left, the couple stood in the kitchen, both very conscious of the presence of God in the room. It was then that Larry heard the clear and unmistakable voice of the Lord, *I have never left you . . . nor have you ever been alone.* Immediately he experienced an inexplicable and overwhelming knowledge that flooded his whole being. From that day on, he felt at home in God's presence. He knew in his heart that he was no longer an orphan and felt at home in his Father's house.

The Orphan Spirit

I believe the orphan spirit is a crippling and common issue of believers who struggle with passivity, unworthiness and low self-esteem. Having an orphan mentality is feeling as though one never belongs or has never been totally accepted by God.

Oh, I know many of us with the orphan spirit believe the Bible and have put our faith in Jesus Christ, but there is still that missing piece—we just do not feel totally at home in the Father's house. We still feel we need to do other things to measure up. We are trapped in the mindset that we have to earn our heavenly Father's love and acceptance. It is difficult to have faith, confidence and zeal toward God when we feel like orphans. Therefore, it is easy for us to live in a *que sera* (whatever will be) mode, because we feel no place of comfort, belonging or protection. We feel lonely and isolated.

If we live life as orphans, we can be saved, born again, pray for everyone we see and make great sacrifices for the ministry, but still stay in agreement with Satan's lie that we do not belong in the Father's house. I now recognize that this was one of my problems. I recall times long after being called to the ministry that I would look in the mirror and berate myself—feeling like a failure, far apart from God. Intellectually, I knew I was a child of God and was called to serve Him, but I still felt unaccepted. I saw God as a master instead of a loving Father. I was striving for approval and not enjoying the fact that He had already accepted me. Looking back, I feel a lot of this stemmed from my own father. He was such a workaholic that he made me feel as though I had no value unless I was working.

This is where passivity comes in. If we are the victims of an orphan spirit, we feel as though we do not have a safe and secure place in the Father's heart. We feel no place of comfort, protection, belonging or affection. Because we feel lonely and isolated, we strive to earn everything we get in life—resulting in insecurity, fear and frustration that put us on a treadmill of unworthiness. Battling feelings of unworthiness, we yield to passivity and then give up, staying stuck in our dysfunction.

If we feel like spiritual orphans, we take one of two paths. We may rebel and say to ourselves, *I'll be my own god; I don't need anyone else. Since I'm an orphan and God doesn't accept me, I'll just do my own thing.* We think that since God is not totally satisfied with us anyway, we might as well go ahead and be disobedient. It is kind of as though we have eaten one cookie and feel bad about it, so we go ahead and eat the whole bag. Then we reason further, *What's the use of going to church? I've failed God too much.*

Or we may take an opposite approach and determine to earn God's acceptance by getting wrapped up in "spiritual" activity. We reason that if we perform enough or do enough, God will finally accept us. Of course, this only medicates our loss until the true revelation that God has accepted us becomes reality. Until then, we seem to live on that treadmill of unworthiness—always exhausted, always looking over our shoulder, afraid of experiencing more rejection. Often, even when others acknowledge or compliment us, we reject it because we do not feel on the inside that we are accepted. We have been so badly damaged that we have trouble experiencing love and acceptance. This is true of most orphan mentalities.

If we choose to live as orphans, we do not have a home. The late Jack Frost, founder of Shiloh Place Ministries, said that we start looking for love in all the wrong places and chasing counterfeit affections. He lists what he calls the "4 Ps" as counterfeit affections: *passions of the flesh, possessions, position* and *power*. *Passions of the flesh* are things that comfort the flesh. If people are not secure in their heavenly Father, they will bond to something else that gives them "rest" and comfort. These passions of the flesh are often in the form of addictions. Some people turn to *possessions*, thinking safety and security lie in those. For others, their *position* and the praise it brings make them feel accepted. And then there is *power*, the feeling of being in control and not needing anyone or anything. For some, that brings a counterfeit satisfaction.

What a victory it is when we finally recognize that God has defined us not by our performance, but rather by His nature in us—and now He calls us His sons and daughters.

Jesus Promised Not to Leave Us Orphans

Look what Jesus promised us in John 14:16–18:

> And I will pray the Father, and He will give you another Helper, that He may abide with you forever—the Spirit of

truth, whom the world cannot receive, because it neither sees Him nor knows Him; but you know Him, for He dwells with you and will be in you. I will not leave you orphans; I will come to you.

It is noteworthy that He said, "I will come to you," because as orphans we feel so abandoned that we do not have the faith to come to the Father on our own. Unworthiness has become a stronghold. We do not have faith in anyone to meet our needs. An orphan spirit cannot be cast out, because it is based on ungodly beliefs developed over a lifetime. It must be replaced by a revelation of the Father's love for us. God says He will disclose Himself to us (see John 14:21). He will make known His love to us in the most intimate way. He also tells us that He will make His home in us. "If anyone loves Me, he will keep My word; and My Father will love him, and We will come to him and make Our home with him" (John 14:23).

Here is the key to overcoming the orphan spirit: It is all about receiving and giving love. God has a mission in mind, that this entire world would experience His love, love that is seen flowing through us, that we give to every person we meet. Jesus said, "A new commandment I give to you, that you love one another. . . . By this all will know that you are My disciples, if you have love for one another" (John 13:34–35).

Once we know we are sons and not orphans, then we know the stronghold of unworthiness is broken. We not only receive love, but we also willingly receive correction. "If you endure chastening, God deals with you as with sons; for what son is there whom a father does not chasten?" (Hebrews 12:7). We know that God has our best interests and growth in mind. As His sons, we are no longer living for our own agenda. We are in submission to His plan. "Shall we not much more readily be in subjection to the Father of spirits and live?" (Hebrews 12:9). The word *subjection* means to get underneath and push up. In other words, we are subject to His mission! We want a part in making His mission successful.

Malachi prophesied:

> Behold I will send you Elijah the prophet
> Before the coming of the great and dreadful day of
>   the LORD.
> And he will turn
> The hearts of the fathers to the children,
> And the hearts of the children to their fathers,
> Lest I come and strike the earth with a curse.
>
> Malachi 4:5–6

The great need in the world today is the need for fathers and a fathering spirit. We no longer need to be orphans ourselves. We need to be at home in our Father's house so we can become fathers to this generation. We want those around us to know that they are not alone or abandoned.

The Victim Spirit

This brings us to the subject of the victim spirit, which I believe also leads people to exhibit a passive personality. Passive people nearly always have stories to tell of how others have taken advantage of them.

Arthur Burk has been criticized for some of the more controversial aspects of his teachings, but I believe he has a clear grasp of what it means to be a victim. Many passive people have what he calls a victim spirit—wherein the person always ends up in a scenario where they get the short end of the stick. As we watch such people go through life, they seem trapped in an endless cycle of abuse.

In his book *Overcoming the Victim Spirit: A Message of Hope*, Burk details six faces of the victim spirit: injustice, dishonor, destruction, malpractice, devouring and defilement. They look like this:

1. *Injustice*: Victims who always seem to get a raw deal no matter what.
2. *Dishonor*: Victims who are wrongly accused, attacked and dishonored no matter how faithful their attempts to do the right thing.
3. *Destruction*: Victims who have freak accidents that are not their fault, seemingly for no reason.
4. *Malpractice*: Victims who are abused in treatment by doctor after doctor.
5. *Devouring*: Victims who have things stolen from them, experience faulty repairs on property and have businesses refuse to honor their warranties.
6. *Defilement*: Victims who have experienced repeated sexual harassment and have no one willing to defend them.

Burk goes on to state:

These are the many faces of a victim. While everyone hits a pothole in the road now and then, victims seem to hit them much more often than others. While any two or three incidents can be written off as part of the reality of living in a world under the curse, some people have too much of what the world calls "bad luck" to be able to ignore it. In reality, there is a whole genre of demons whose job it is to create victims. I ministered once to a woman who had been in an abusive marriage until her husband died of cancer. She then married a fine man who quickly began to abuse her. She asked me, "Do I have a sign hanging around my neck saying, 'Come abuse me'?" I assured her she did. It was not visible in the natural but one part of the victim spirit's job is to be a flashing beacon in the spirit realm, attracting the attention of all predator demons. Once a predator demon has made connections with a victim demon, the two demons facilitate bringing their human hosts together in a damaging way. The other half of the victim spirit's job is to persuade the human victim that there is nothing that can be done to change the situation. They eventually arrive at the conclusion that in some way or another, the recurring problems are their fault, and that they just need to lower their expectations in life and endure what comes.[1]

There are a great many people who love God and are used by Him—yet who also are still vulnerable to a victim spirit that holds them back. But thank God no one has to continue to live this way! We can identify this victim demon and command it to leave us. God has called us to walk in freedom and victory.

Victims see and experience life through a filter in which external influences control them and trigger emotional responses. They need to possess an internal stability based on truth instead. Looking through victim glasses, we always see with a distortion—it looks as though our happiness and peace are based on our current circumstances and on how loved, affirmed and accepted we feel. If our positive emotions are fed, we are happy. If we do not feel adequately affirmed and validated, we feel rejected, devalued or like a failure. Then our negative emotions take over, and we descend into a pit. No matter what happens in life, we find a way to play the victim. We may be completely blind to the mind trap that binds us, yet keenly aware that happiness and peace are always elusive and evasive.

One would think that living a victim life is an easy road, considering that most victims never see their role of responsibility in a relationship. They are masters at seeing faults in others and tend to blame others for whatever is wrong. They are always looking for the "perfect" person who will ride in on a white horse and rescue them from their life of misery, defeat and insecurity. But, as with any faulty thinking patterns, victim thinking robs us of a life of freedom and abundance. As victims, we are guilty of giving away our personal power to others by not being assertive in our relationships.

1. Arthur Burk, *Overcoming the Victim Spirit: A Message of Hope* (Whittier, Calif.: Plumbline Ministries, 2001), 9–10.

As believers, though, we are not powerless to change our thinking, our attitudes, our habits and our lives. When we begin to see ourselves as God sees us, we can break free from a victim spirit. We have a choice: "I have set before you life and death, blessing and cursing; therefore choose life, that both you and your descendants may live" (Deuteronomy 30:19).

We can choose life! We can choose to take responsibility for our own lives, allowing the Lord to break up our mental concrete and transform us. We do not have to stay in the prison of a victim mentality. We do not have to continue believing the enemy's lies. We do not have to continue to give ourselves and our personal power away. We can stop this cycle of defeat.

God has created each of us with an inherent value. The worth and value God our Creator has assigned to us does not change. Whether others approve of us, like us, reject us or criticize us, nothing changes who God created us to be. No matter what we have been through, our value does not change.

Jesus Christ has already paid the price for our freedom. If we are living as victims, then we are believing and living a lie. A lie that goes unchallenged becomes the truth we live by. If we allow the Lord to let His healing power flow, we can experience change. Then we can begin to experience the peace, love, joy and stability that are part of the abundant life!

If we do not deal with our feelings of being victims or orphans, in the long term we risk continuing to live as wounded people, which is what we will explore next.

5

Wounded People

How do we become Ahabs or Jezebels? Why do we act the way we act? How do these patterns become so established? One thing we know is that our greatest desire is to be loved and our greatest fear is rejection. Everyone is broken to some extent, but God has made provision for all of us—not only for the forgiveness of our sins, but for our total healing. Jesus said, "He has sent Me to heal the brokenhearted, to proclaim liberty to the captives" (Luke 4:18). Learning how to overcome our difficulties and enjoy spiritual freedom and good emotional health is not only a journey, but an ongoing process. God is glorified as we seek Him for truth in body, soul and spirit. "Behold, You desire truth in the inward parts, and in the hidden part You will make me to know wisdom" (Psalm 51:6).

When we refuse to deal with the passive traits we have looked at so far—self-defeat, rejection, rebellion, a victim mentality or an orphan spirit—we can become wounded people. Wounded people build walls around themselves, and the thickness of their walls correlates with the depth of their wounds. For example, if a girl has an abusive mother and then marries a husband who is abusive, gradually her behavior either becomes passive or aggressive. She will live as if she deserves to be treated poorly and has come to expect nothing else, or else she will live in a strike-first, attack mode.

Defensiveness also can come into play. It is an oversensitive response rooted in the fear of rejection. When asked a simple question such as, "Have you seen my keys?" a defensive person might respond, "I didn't take them!" Deeply wounded people almost always display more emotional reactivity. They often either express or suppress anger (rage), even to the point of becoming depressed or anxious. In extreme cases they are suicidal or homicidal.

Wounded and insecure people also interpret any type of correction as rejection. If you dare to point out an inconsistency in their lives, they may attack you. Their wounds are so deep that in effect they say inaudibly (probably subconsciously), but with their exaggerated responses, *I will never again experience the pain of rejection.* Any correction spoken into their lives is usually interpreted as more rejection.

Fear of abandonment is also an issue for wounded people and may result in panic and anxiety attacks. As Tim Clinton and Gary Sibcy say in their book *Attachments: Why You Love, Feel, and Act the Way You Do*:

> Fear of abandonment is the fundamental human fear. It is so basic and so profound that it emerges even before we develop a language to describe it. It is so powerful that it activates our body's autonomic nervous system, causing our hearts to race, our breathing to become shallow and rapid, our stomachs to quiver, and our hands to shake. We feel a sense of panic that will not be assuaged until we are close to our caregivers—until we regain a feeling of security.[1]

1. Tim Clinton and Gary Sibcy, *Attachments: Why You Love, Feel, and Act the Way You Do* (Brentwood, Tenn.: Integrity, 2002), 22.

Both Jezebel and Ahab were wounded people. That much they had in common. However, their behaviors could not have been more different. When we exhibit Jezebel-like or Ahab-like behaviors, our wounds show up in dramatically different ways.

Jezebel the Narcissist

Jezebels are extremely narcissistic. They are self-serving. Because of their wounds, they live without concern for the damage that they cause. The world is all about them. They are never wrong. If they apologize, it is only to say, "I'm sorry you misunderstood me," or "I'm sorry you got your feelings hurt," or "I'm sorry your face got in the way of my fist"—but never do they take responsibility and admit that anything is their fault. They also hate change and resist it.

Jezebels live in a conscious attack mode, reasoning, *I've been hurt, so I will not be hurt again.* Jezebels are never thankful, and their attitude is that the world is here to serve them. Jezebels will always get their needs met in an unhealthy way. They usually have such low self-worth that they tend to partner with someone passive who believes that he or she is a bad person. That is why these Jezebel and Ahab personalities always seem to end up together. A Jezebel (male or female) will find a passive Ahab match who is looking for identity so much that he or she will almost "welcome" the abuse inherent in such a relationship.

Ahab the Martyr

Ahabs, on the other hand, come across as selfless, but are also very selfish (it is just more hidden, so they look good to others). They live like victims or martyrs. The ultimate Ahabs draw all the attention to themselves, and they often stay in a marriage because of the children. They are selfish in a marriage because they manage very early on to get the children to volunteer as their emotional support system. They end up pulling energy from the kids, holding them as emotional hostages because the children are "forced" for their own well-being to emotionally support the passive parent, who claims to be the victim. Selfish Ahabs allow their partners to take advantage of them (appearing selfless), and yet draw their children into taking sides and taking on the role of supporters.

Jesus Christ was a victim by choice—and there is therefore no need for anyone else to be a victim. He suffered for us all and by His sacrifice justified us, making provision for all things, so we are never justified in acting as a victim. Therefore the passive person who acts like a victim—trying to redo and reinvent the cross—flies in the face of God. As one wise but unidentified person said, "Using others to stop our pain is the height of passivity."

We have no right to declare ourselves victims, but must acknowledge instead that Christ was the ultimate victim. Then we have to take responsibility for our lives and declare His ability and power to deliver us.

We Ahabs consciously give power away, but from a state of woundedness. We give our power away in order for the other person to validate our identities and to tell us who we are. We think, *If I love you enough, you will love me*, and we look for a partner who will tell us we are worthy and lovable.

It flies in the face of God for a passive person to give someone else the power to tell them they are worthy. Worth comes from God alone and from being created in His image. No person can take away someone else's identity in Christ, but Ahabs usually attack their own identities, believing whatever Jezebels say to them.

Ahab and Jezebel Differences

We hear a great deal about Jezebels in our society. Let me reemphasize that these personalities have no gender. However, the aggressive Jezebel spirit does operate differently through a man than it does through a woman.

God has given women a gift in their emotions. They are intuitive and usually come across as far more sensitive than men. Therefore, the enemy of their souls tries to take advantage of this giftedness and tempts women to use their emotions illegitimately to get their way, often through manipulation.

On the other hand, God has gifted men as leaders. They possess strength and can offer protection. But the enemy then comes along and deceptively lures men into controlling others through domination and intimidation. If a man is insecure, he illegitimately uses his strength to control his wife, his environment and the people and situations around him.

I believe there are far more passive Ahabs in society than aggressive Jezebels. Of the two, the Ahabs are far more likely to change, be they men or women. A true, bona fide Jezebel of either gender rarely changes. Jezebels do not want to change because they are quite comfortable with their lifestyle! However, Ahabs are very uncomfortable with their lives because they are not experiencing intimacy, yet they sense a strong need for connection—whether in a marriage, a friendship, a church situation, with a co-worker or in any other relationship.

The question of willingness to change has something to do with a person's comfort level and how motivated they are to change it. However, it can also be examined in the light of how wounded a person is and whether demonic activity is present. For example, many times wounds are so deep in a Jezebel that the thick walls he or she has built seemingly never will come down.

Often demonic strongholds are present in both Ahabs and Jezebels. Demonic activity results from vows and judgments such people have made against those who have wounded them, often their parents. A door is opened through their vows, and the enemy has an "invitation" to come into their situation through lack of forgiveness. A demon will join with a person in a vow of hatred or bitterness they have made toward someone who has hurt or disappointed them. One result is that Ahabs and Jezebels become just like their parents, or just the opposite. Obviously, the key to deliverance from such a demonic stronghold lies in genuine repentance from the vows and judgments.

The good news is that an Ahab's answer is within. Ahabs have the power necessary to call for wholeness in a relationship if they will deal with their own dysfunction. Ahabs need to get to the place where they draw good boundaries, deciding that they are not going to live a passive, paralyzed life anymore. The bottom line is that when Ahabs confront themselves first, they get out of the cycle of abuse.

Once an Ahab does that, it is up to his or her partner to change and not stay stuck in a place of unhealthy communication and unhappiness. If an Ahab chooses not to continue his or her behavior in a dysfunctional relationship, it can sometimes result in separation or divorce, as it did with Paul and Cindy in chapter 3. But if the other partner then recognizes that he or she was wrong, misses the Ahab and wants to work on the issues and pursue intimacy, that is wonderful. If this is not the case, then the recovering Ahab knows that he or she is becoming well, whole and ready to move on with life.

Jezebels, however, rarely have any intention of changing—and they usually do not. Typically they are so wounded that they refuse to take responsibility for anything and are "content" to remain as they are. Between their low-self esteem and inflated ego, their pride keeps them from admitting just how wounded they are. They go through life manipulating people and situations and making everything everyone else's fault. It is an extremely difficult pattern to break unless a Jezebel completely submits to the authority of Christ and agrees to work wholeheartedly toward change.

Passive Parents

Ultimately it is the passive parent, the more uncomfortable one, who causes the most damage to a child. He or she does not urge the aggressive parent, the more selfish one, to come into balance, which then throws all the parent-child dynamics off balance, too. As I said earlier, the passive parent often turns to the kids for emotional support, and the kids miss connecting with the aggressive parent because they are always focused on the needs of the passive parent.

A child caught in the middle between Ahab and Jezebel parents does not feel protected, but is totally vulnerable. He or she may be abused by the aggressive parent and then feel anger toward the passive parent for not being protective. The child may become Ahab-like as a result—or a Jezebel personality can form in the child when the child is not protected by the passive parent. Jezebel personalities appear to form from extremely inconsistent, ambivalent parenting—such as when a parent switches from warm to cold behavior in an attempt to get his or her own needs met. In Christian clinical circles, this is sometimes associated with the terms *disorganized relationship style* or *borderline personality trait*.

Borderline personalities revolve around unstable relationships, a poor sense of self, mood swings and impulsivity. Such individuals intensely fear abandonment and become clingy, needy and helpless. They immediately attach to others, and then they push the same people away to avoid rejection. Their relationships are cyclical, with repeating patterns of intense neediness and then backpedaling. Simply stated, their mindset is one of "I hate you—don't leave me!"

The modeling of such unbalanced parents, especially passive parents, damages a child's ability to grow up and form healthy, assertive relationships. Children who see adults model healthy behavior and process their emotions in a healthy way, however, are likely to avoid the extremes of passivity and aggressiveness and grow up assertive and whole—capable of establishing and maintaining intimate relationships.

Passive People Seek Help

Numerous counselors have told me that passive people are usually the ones who seek therapy. They usually come in and say that their partner is treating them inappropriately, with disrespect, bashing them and putting them down. They not only want that behavior to stop, but they are desperately seeking intimacy and connection.

Aggressive people, on the other hand, rarely seek help because they see no need to change. They are accusatory, blaming and complaining about the other partner—believing they have no fault. They are all about themselves. They do not want to do relationships. Their woundedness is about avoiding intimacy and connection at all costs. They are content to live without intimacy and have no inclination to change anything. Therefore, it is the passive person in such a relationship who is desperate for connection and will seek help.

Many therapists believe that starting by age two and going up to age seven, the way in which a child deals with anger will determine whether that child will become an adult who is codependent or dependent. Codependents will most likely end up in a relationship where they seek their identity and validity from their spouses, and will stay in a cycle of abuse—trying to feel accepted. However, dependent people will seek their identity and fulfillment from something beyond their relationship such as their career or level of success. They may be either unhappy or content in their relationships, but either way, they can always fill their emotional tanks by achieving things outside the realm of their personal relationships.

Peacekeepers or Peacemakers

Passive people are usually the peacekeepers. In other words, their goal is peace at any price. They choose not to confront and will quickly brush away any thought of standing up for truth in a situation because of the fear of conflict. They will not be honest about their emotions and usually will blame themselves or figure an issue does not matter that much. Not confronting an issue will result in short-term gratification and only temporary peace.

Healthy people, on the other hand, will be peacemakers. They will recognize their God-given identity and authority and be willing to assertively confront a person with whom they are in conflict. At first this can be uncomfortable, but because healthy people respect themselves and their God-given identity, long-term peace will result.

Passive people will not take up their God-given freedom. They refuse to step up, become assertive, say what they need to and command respect. Then they blame others for taking away their freedom, when in reality they have chosen to give it away. The passive person must step up to the plate, stop blaming an abuser and say, "This is what I need. This is what you can no longer do. Let's work toward having a healthy relationship."

When you deal with a Jezebel personality, it does not seem to matter what course of action you take, because they do not take responsibility or blame for anything. If you take action concerning something, they will blame you; if you do not take action, they will blame you. You never win. Jezebels are very slick, always excusing themselves from any responsibility.

Meanwhile, an Ahab will go on taking full responsibility for a Jezebel's actions as well as his or her own. But this is an alliance with evil, as I said before. My friend Paul was in spiritual trouble when he put the fear of his wife, Cindy, above the fear of God. For a long time, he gave his freedom and authority in Christ away to her rather than honoring God by becoming the person God created him to be. Eventually Paul knew he had to change from being a peacekeeper who sought peace at any price to being a peacemaker who would stand up in his God-given identity and seek long-term results. That meant he needed to face Cindy head-on, tell her what he needed and ask her to change, too. The difficulty involved in seeking change in a Jezebel is no excuse for an Ahab not to seek spiritual and professional help.

Critically Wounded

Joni had a terrible past and a terrible upbringing. I do not think I have ever met someone who was so wounded. Her parents had been members of a religious cult and had strange views about God. She was sexually and physically abused and received absolutely no love or affirmation growing up. She married into an abusive relationship, and finally, after having multiple children, was divorced.

Because of her extreme wounding, Joni has a major rejection complex. The problem is that no one can speak truth to her—she cannot hear it. It is difficult to talk to her because she interprets everything as rejection. If you ever disagree or contradict what she wants to hear or think, she converts to an attack mode and there is serious trouble. Even if someone does not answer the phone, she interprets it as more rejection and accuses the person of all kinds of things. Her response is to attack anyone she feels might speak truth to her, but she takes no responsibility for her behavior. Then she always reverts back to justifying her behavior—spiritualizing her anger and her fleshly outbursts. If she does not get her way, she manipulates with tears and emotional breakdowns, creating a lot of drama. She does whatever she can to manipulate other people. Although she always demands that everyone show her sympathy, she can be hardcore on everyone else. Joni says she wants the truth, but in reality she cannot handle it.

Ultimately, Joni and wounded people like her just want to be loved—but they repel the very people they are trying to get to love them. They fish for compliments, and every time they walk into a room, they want to be seen and noticed. If they perceive that they are unnoticed, they become offended. They often have an emotional addiction to someone (or an obsession), continually trying to force that person to love them and take pity on them. Often people this wounded are sexually addicted because they interpret sex as love.

Joni talks incessantly, but she just wants someone to be her ear—to hear her vent. But she will not let anyone be a voice to speak into her life. She displays a chronic spirit of neediness, where she has to be the center of attention.

In so many of these types of people with rejection, they feel they can do or say anything they want, but they insist that you respond to them in love! They more or less say, "Let me vent and spew all my venom, but you sit there and take it and sympathize with my sick perspective." Additionally, they are suspicious of everyone. Whenever there is a disagreement with someone, they not only try to attack the person, but they try to collect as many people as they can to get on board with them and agree that the other person is bad.

Such people are also usually addicted to drama. They cannot seem to deal with peace and quiet, so they create drama. It is not uncommon for them to start fights—usually over something irrelevant—only to say (consciously or subconsciously) that they are not getting enough attention. They want to perpetuate the drama.

If you let people who are wounded this severely do something for you, then they own you! You will never hear the end of it. They will use guilt, condemnation and threats to get a payback for the favor they did for you. Usually it is a favor they suggested in the first place because they want you to feel obligated to them.

What confuses many is that those who manifest such an aggressive and controlling Jezebel personality can be what I call spiritually schizophrenic. On the one hand they show a spiritual side, but then at any point they can change personalities—first they talk about how they are "used of God" and are following Him, then they go ballistic, attacking someone.

This reminds me of Peter when Jesus praised his response to the question, "Who do you say that I am?" Peter answered, "You are the Christ, the Son of the living God." But moments later, when Jesus spoke of His impending crucifixion, Peter responded in a fleshly outburst, saying, "Far be it from You, Lord; this shall not happen to You!" (Matthew 16:15–16, 22).

Jesus rebuked Peter, saying, "Get behind Me, Satan! You are an offense to Me, for you are not mindful of the things of God, but the things of men" (verse 23).

Peter flipped from one extreme to the other in a matter of minutes. Critically wounded people often behave like that, intensely spiritual one minute and quite the opposite the next.

If critically wounded people such as Joni do allow themselves to hear and absorb the truth, then they recognize they must change. They realize that the responsibility for change is on them, yet they do not want to change because they do not want to go through the painful process of facing the truth and receiving healing. If they refuse to hear the truth, then they are destined to stay stuck in their woundedness and continue to blame everyone else (including the devil) for what is wrong in their lives.

Scripture makes it clear that ultimately the solution to our problems is up to us. Whatever our upbringing or our past, we have to be teachable and receive the healing that God has provided. "Make straight paths for your feet, so that what is lame may not be dislocated, but rather be healed" (Hebrews 12:13).

Passivity Also Leads to Rage

Wounded Jezebels are not the only ones who allow themselves to turn their wounds into rage. When passive Ahabs refuse to set boundaries, their anger also turns to rage. Depression also sets in because they never deal with the feelings they stuff away. When feelings are not properly processed, a person becomes passive-aggressive and can be like a ticking bomb ready to explode.

Passive people usually do not forgive themselves and even have issues with God. They become blind to God's ability to make them whole. They often have a mindset that flies in the face of God—that the blood of Jesus was not enough to handle their sins and heal their issues. They feel they are somehow a special case, and are both enraged about it and proud of it.

Yet for all that, Ahab-like people still often look good externally because they take so much abuse and internalize so much anger. Most of us have met a passive person who is more or less saying, "Look at what a good person I am to stay in a marriage with that horrible person." In the next chapter, we will look more in depth at how a passive nature that punctures and wounds us plays out in our marriage relationships.

6

Passivity in Marriage

Jim was the pastor of a church in a sleepy town in the eastern United States. He and his wife, Linda, had founded the church, enjoying its steady growth over many years. As Jim approached the golden years of his ministry, he knew it was time to "pass the baton" and turn the helm of the church over to his son, Michael, who was also an ordained minister and had worked with his dad for many years. They had frequent conversations about the upcoming decision. Finally, after delaying his decision for two years, Jim agreed that it was time to turn the church over to Michael.

The problem was, Linda (to whom Jim had abdicated his authority years earlier) did not agree because she wanted to stay right there in her position in the church, which not only gave her an identity but a sense of power. Michael was aware of how his mom controlled his dad, so he insisted on a meeting where his dad's decision would be shared with the elders and deacons and the minutes would be recorded. The following Sunday, Jim stood before the congregation to announce his decision and ask the church to now recognize

Michael as the senior pastor. His intentions were complete and explicit.

Interestingly, Linda was not in the service that Sunday morning. In fact, Jim had told Michael months earlier that when he talked to Linda about "handing the baton" to Michael, she told him, "You can do what you want, but I'm not leaving this church and my position here." It became obvious that she was the controller and Jim was passive. It seems likely that her friends in the congregation would have filled her in even though she was not present on that important Sunday. But she would neither face nor hear the truth, and her husband had adopted the role of Ahab by withholding the truth from her, so great was his fear of her reaction.

Soon after Jim's public announcement, the whole situation began to unravel. Michael dutifully took his place as senior pastor of the church, but before long, word began to filter back to him through various members that he had "stolen" the church from his dad. When he confronted his dad, Jim acknowledged that Michael's allegations were true—that he and his wife were indeed telling people in the community that Michael had stolen the church from them. Immediately Michael disagreed and reminded his dad, "That's not true; you turned the church over to me!"

Through his passivity, Jim had set up conflict within his family. He had sandwiched himself between his son, to whom he had relinquished leadership of the church, and his wife, to whom he had relinquished his God-given authority. As unbelievable as it sounds, this man truly feared his wife's reaction so much that he withheld the truth from her. Even though he knew she was not on board with him, he deceptively stepped out on a limb and exerted his authority as pastor by turning the church over to his son. Then he backtracked because he knew she would bring down the hammer. Sadly, because of the fear of her reaction, he pretended like passing the baton had never happened.

Jim's passivity was mind-boggling. He had even told Michael at one point that he could recall the specific day years earlier when he had given his leadership away to his wife and that he had regretted it ever since (but had never reclaimed it). The bottom line was that Jim would not deal with his wife and had abdicated his authority to her. Rather than have the backbone to stand up to her, he chose to alienate his own son and the rest of his family by turning the church against Michael.

Michael tried every way he knew to get his dad to accept the truth and refused to compromise with his dad by giving in to the lie. He could have simply given the church back to his dad, but he refused to be passive and chose to stand for truth. At the same time, he desperately wanted his relationship with his parents to be restored.

Jim came to Michael on more than one occasion and said, "Can't we just forget the past and go on with our lives?" But Michael wisely would say, "But, Dad, you are asking me to agree with a lie, and I just can't do that." He willingly forgave his parents, but he refused to line up with their lies about how the change in the senior pastorate had taken place.

However, Jim behaved so passively, fearing the consequences of telling Linda the truth, that he was totally paralyzed in dealing with the damage he had caused. Linda was under the influence of a Jezebel spirit, but the bigger problem was that Jim refused to confront it and deal with it. Tragically, he alienated himself from his son, his family, his church and his grandchildren all because he was afraid of standing up to his wife. Jim created a quagmire by refusing to be truthful. His passivity destroyed trust, confidence and years of enjoying his family.

Hidden and Not-So-Hidden Agendas

How do people like Jim and Linda get trapped in dysfunctional marriage relationships? In his book *Getting the Love*

You Want: A Guide for Couples (Henry Holt, 1988), Harville Hendrix explains his discovery of the *imago* (from the word *image*). Basically, the imago is when one or both people in a relationship have an unconscious agenda for their partner, looking to the partner to complete any "unfinished business" with them left over from their childhood. Therefore, they put an unreasonable demand on the partner to do something that the partner is incapable of doing—giving them what they did not get from their major childhood caretakers. Hendrix says:

> What we are doing, I have discovered from years of theoretical research and clinical observation, is looking for someone who has the predominant character traits of the people who raised us. Our old brain (the part of the brain that carries suppressed memories), trapped in the eternal now, and having only a dim awareness of the outside world, is trying to re-create the environment of childhood. And the reason the old brain is trying to resurrect it is not a matter of habit or blind compulsion, but of a compelling need to heal old childhood wounds. The ultimate reason you fell in love with your mate, I am suggesting, is not that your mate was young and beautiful, had an impressive job, had a "point value" equal to yours, or had a kind disposition. You fell in love because your old brain had your partner confused with your parents! Your old brain believed that it had actually found the ideal candidate to make up for the psychological and emotional damage you experienced in childhood. . . .
>
> Many people have a hard time accepting the idea that they have searched for partners that resemble their caretakers. On a conscious level they were looking for people with only positive traits—people who were kind, loving, good-looking, intelligent and creative. In fact, if they had an unhappy childhood they may have deliberately searched for people who were radically different from their caretakers.[1]

1. Harville Hendrix, Ph.D., *Getting the Love You Want: A Guide for Couples* (New York: Henry Holt Company, 1988), 14, 34.

Many times people make a vow in their hearts and tell themselves, *I'll never marry someone controlling like my father*, or *I'll never be married to a control freak like my mother*. However, it seems that no matter how they determine this, most people are drawn to mates who have the same negative or positive traits their childhood caretakers had. Sadly, most people seem to choose a partner with more of the negative traits.

Two Passive Housewives

I saw this concept come to life in Amy, a woman who had been married for eight years. When Amy came to me, she was emotionally bankrupt and depleted. She lamented about how after years of centering her life on her husband, John, she was receiving nothing in return. Everything was focused on making his life easier and accomplishing his goals. She finally reached the end of herself and declared to him that her emotional tank was empty and he was going to have to step up to the plate. She had let him make withdrawals from her emotional bank, but he never once made any deposits into it. He had overdrawn the account with her, and she was depleted.

Of course, the first thing I pointed out to her was that she had waited far too long to act, which she readily admitted. But like many newlyweds, she was convinced from the beginning that she could fix him. She thought that if she just continued to show John unconditional love, he would eventually give that back to her. But it never happened. Any time Amy would express her needs in the marriage, John would selfishly ignore her emotional plea and make everything about him and his needs.

Amy's problem was that she was the self-appointed fixer. Her father was an extremely self-centered, abusive alcoholic. According to the imago concept, she was guilty of unconsciously trying to fix her dad by fixing her husband. If she did not recognize this, she would most likely end up losing her present relationship and entering another one in which she would try to fix someone else.

Subconsciously, Amy had found a husband who, although he was not an alcoholic like her father, was equally self-centered and self-serving. In trying to fix John—and subconsciously fixing her unfinished business with her dad through him—she wore herself out. In reality, she was trying to fix John not for his sake, but for her—in order to stop her unconscious pain from childhood. Now, however, Amy had reached the point where she found her dysfunctional relationship with her husband repulsive.

As Hendrix points out about imago, in reality only 20 percent of Amy's problem was about her life with John, while 80 percent was about her mom never fixing her dad. The majority of Amy's behavior was like her mother's past behavior, and she was trying to fix her husband for the wrong reasons. If Amy stayed in her disabled condition, she might lose John, only to marry someone just like him again.

As Amy repented of her passivity and began to confront her husband, he seemed to have no clue about their issues, saying, "I think I'm a nice guy." He had no comprehension of her needs, other than how she might change to make life more pleasing for him. Sadly, neither of them was calling the other to wholeness and holiness.

It is the purpose of God and part of our God-given function to call one another to wholeness instead of rewounding each other. Amy had to make a decision not only to draw boundaries, but to call John to wholeness, clearly telling him what she needed and standing her ground. She also had to repent of her passivity and of being her husband's fixer. Only as she respected herself did their marriage have a chance.

Again, Amy's greatest mistake was waiting far too long to confront John. Passive people avoid confrontation and become peacekeepers instead of peacemakers. Peacekeepers passively settle for temporary relief (short-term gratification). They reason, *If I ignore this, it will go away*, or *Maybe something will change*. Peacemakers assertively insist on long-term gratification, which involves the work of confronting issues honestly and blatantly. Once Amy became healthy, she was able to do that, telling her husband that she could longer function in a one-sided relationship.

John and Amy's marriage did begin to fall apart. She had tried so hard to please him, but had finally reached her limit and explained to him that she could not go on. He then blamed her for not insisting sooner that they seek counseling. He also blamed her for not making him seek treatment for his depression. Of course, if she had taken that action earlier, he would have labeled her as paranoid and pushy.

It seemed like a no-win situation for Amy, and their dysfunction still continues. Currently John is getting counseling and has had his medications adjusted. However, he is steadfast in his refusal to take responsibility and is paranoid and pushy about their relationship. He still refuses to acknowledge his extreme self-centeredness and his one-sided approach to life. In his eyes, it is all about him.

The bottom line is that controllers like John will always twist things around to seem like someone else's fault. It goes back to the Garden of Eden again, where Adam took no responsibility for his action, blaming both God and "the woman You gave me" (see Genesis 3).

Sharon was another passive housewife trying to please her husband. When I talked to Sharon, her first frustration was that as long as she did not say anything to disagree with Ted in any way and gave him sex whenever he wanted, everything was fine. However, she told me she was dying inside. Everything in life was centered on building up Ted's ego.

Ted obviously had issues with extreme insecurity and inferiority. His inflated ego was out of control. When they were out with other couples, every reference he made about his wife was a sexual innuendo. He also began to hide all their money, making her ask him for permission to spend money even for something as small as a sandwich. At home he increasingly scolded the kids over nothing and upset them. Then when the younger one would cry, Ted would call him a crybaby.

Things escalated even more as Ted began to imply that Sharon was unfaithful and check her cell phone records. However, Sharon told me at one point that as bad as things were, rather than leave the marriage, she would put up with everything because she could not bear the possibility of Ted marrying someone else who would then partially mother her kids.

Sharon was living a lie. For the sake of temporary peace, she passively stayed trapped in her marriage. She was not only extremely unhappy, but was stuffing her emotions. Consciously, Sharon said she could not live that way any longer, but unconsciously she felt as if she did not deserve anything better and that her love could change Ted. She was addicted to misery.

I told Sharon it was time that she become assertive, stop enabling Ted's behavior and feeding his ego, and say "enough." It was up to her to tell Ted she could not live that way anymore. Then it would be up to him to decide if he wanted to address his self-serving behavior and inflated ego or lose his wife and children.

Presently, however, Sharon remains fearful of confronting Ted the way she needs to. She is afraid of losing her financial security and is choosing to remain a peacekeeper. She has not taken the assertive stand of laying everything on the table and putting Ted in the position of either choosing her or choosing to continue his selfish behavior.

God Hates Divorce—and Lies

Divorce is rampant in our society and is a difficult subject to talk about. The Bible clearly says that God hates divorce, but the Bible also declares that God hates lying, cheating, manipulation, control, abuse and discord. What is more pleasing to God? Does He call us to stay together to satisfy religious minds and to live a total lie?

I am not condoning divorce in any way; I am against it. I hate the fact that it is so epidemic in our society. But while I do not like divorce, I also realize it is not unforgivable. I do not like sickness either, whether it shows up physically in the body or emotionally in an unhealthy relationship. However, these things happen in life and must be dealt with. If they are not, we wind up living in denial for the sake of religious appearances and never confronting a lie. We bury conflicts and live a lifeless existence that gives no glory to God. Divorce usually occurs because people refuse to deal with their issues. Jesus talked about the reason God allowed Moses to grant divorce—because of hardness of heart (see Mark 10:2–9).

In many marriages, both people surrendered to a stalemate long ago. Have you ever watched such couples having dinner at a restaurant? It is not uncommon to observe that they do not say a word to each other the entire meal. In reality, they are probably emotionally divorced and are only staying together for convenience, or they are afraid to change or be alone. People who are not honest about their relationships are living a lie. Sometimes one partner may try to work at things—but often the other does not want to change.

Decades ago, women in such relationships felt they had no choice but to stay in an abusive relationship because the husband was the breadwinner. By standing up to a husband and refusing to accept verbal or physical abuse, a woman might have faced the risk of ending the marriage and losing her means of support. Sadly, these women stayed in their relationships while their emotions died and they succumbed to passivity—doing nothing, feeling they had no other choice. I do not call that abundant life.

We are imprinted by God for intimacy. If God's call is for us to achieve an intimacy that reflects the Trinity, then in a marriage it is right for the person seeking help to call their partner to wholeness. If that partner refuses, then a decision has to be made about the relationship.

By *wholeness* I mean that both partners (hopefully believers in Christ) live as a unit. But often, one partner chooses to live a lie or live in denial. He or she may refuse to take responsibility when trust is broken or unjustly blame the other person for things, always making issues the other person's fault.

One man told me that to stay married, he would have had to abdicate his divine authority as head of the household to his wife and therefore sacrifice God's call to intimacy with Him. Many in his position take the easy road, trying to meet their immediate needs for peace and acceptance instead of standing on the truth. Just like Esau, they seek immediate gratification and sell their birthright for a meal, so to speak. They meet their immediate needs by selling out on God's call and purpose for their lives. That never leads to wholeness.

Wholeness is a journey and a process—not a destination. When someone is whole, they have an ability to hold on to themselves (what they think and feel), yet intentionally and consciously listen to someone coming from a different point of view and not feel threatened by it. As God calls us to wholeness, we must be willing in our relationships to become more like each other and compromise on different areas. Opposites do attract, and so many opposites end up together. But sometimes one partner either will not or cannot compromise—his or her wounds are too severe. Wholeness only comes where there is a willingness to seek and accept change.

A Passive Husband

George had been miserable from the beginning of his marriage. He dated Melissa for only a few months before marrying her. During their brief courtship she was very unaffectionate, which he attributed to her Christian convictions. However, immediately after their marriage, the lack of affection continued even to the point that she would not let him touch her breasts. This, of course, frustrated him, but when he would try to talk to her about it, she would immediately become angry and aggressive, verbally tearing him to shreds. She would fly into a rage about something insignificant such as the untruths that he did not hang up his clothes or did not help wash the dishes. Melissa would also spend countless hours every day putting on makeup. This would irritate and grieve him because she spent such a huge portion of every day on her primping, while neglecting many other important activities.

Although George knew their relationship was not normal and Melissa was defrauding him, he would always apologize to her and walk away in defeat. Because George was a committed Christian and did not believe in divorce, he did not see any other option. As a passive Ahab, his mentality (subconscious brain programming) was to work even harder to please Melissa. He would always buy her things and make every effort to win her love and respect. Tragically, he continued to live in misery for many years. The more he tried to get her to love him, the less she respected him.

Eventually, after far too many years had passed, Melissa agreed to counseling. Although they spent much money over a long period of time, little was accomplished. She refused to admit that she had once been sexually molested by a family member, and she declared that the counselors who suggested this possibility were not spiritual and could not have heard from God. However, as more things unfolded and the truth surfaced, it was obvious that she had indeed been molested. Ultimately she sued George for divorce, refusing to face her own woundedness.

Looking back, George recognized that he had been far too passive. Trying to be the nice guy and not wanting a divorce, he had given up his own self-respect and capitulated to defeat and even hopelessness. Finally, he recognized his behavior as an Ahab. He discovered the roots of his passivity in his childhood scripting and realized that he should have been far more assertive, establishing boundaries early in the marriage and refusing to live such a defrauded existence.

George now recognized that Melissa had held him mentally and emotionally hostage. She had him "trained," but she was not the first person to train him. His passive mother had first done that. George now admits, "I was acting like my mother. That's why Melissa beat up on me. I was allowing it." Melissa's mindset was that she deserved to have the world wait on her. She was only concerned about her own needs, and she needed (and will find again) someone to buy into that mindset. For years, the wounded part of George believed her accusations that he was in the wrong and that if he tried harder, she would give him what he needed—the validation he never got from his parents.

Melissa is one example of a controller who plays both roles. On the one hand, she wanted to dominate their relationship, but on the other hand she wanted to play the role of the "helpless" wife, with George's role that of the slave there to meet her every need. When George got healthy, she could no longer continue her abusive role. Ultimately she had to get healthy or leave.

Melissa chose to remain the victim and leave the marriage. She blamed all of George's friends, spreading hateful things about each of them. God wanted to heal her and gave her every opportunity for wholeness, but when people like Melissa will not face their own issues, they quickly find someone else to blame. It is easier for them to protect their wounds by blaming others, staying the victim and even blaming God than to admit, as the old spiritual song says, "It's me, it's me, O Lord . . . standing in the need of prayer."

George became more and more spiritually and emotionally healthy when he left behind his passive ways and determined that he would no longer give his power away. Although Melissa became angry at losing her position of control, George began to thrive in self-confidence and self-worth. He recognized his passive patterns, and once he broke free of the Jezebel spirit and defeated the Ahab spirit, he began to enjoy living life again. George broke the curse of passivity in himself, and with courage and determination began to heal and become a more whole and complete person.

Passive Men in Marriage

While many men are domineering and possessive, many have also totally succumbed to passivity. In fact, four words many husbands dread hearing from their wives are, "We need to talk." Many men have the attitude that since they work hard all week, they are justified in feeling tired and saying, "I don't feel like dealing with this," thus abdicating all authority to their wives.

Sometimes Ahab-like men exert no leadership and choose not to deal with conflict because they fear losing sexual intimacy with their wives. One man even asked me why he and his wife had not kissed for years but still engage in frequent sex. When kissing stops, intimacy has stopped. Kissing communicates openness and trust, but some partners live a lie to the point of subconsciously reasoning, *I don't like this person because he or she has hurt me, but I am staying in the relationship and ignoring the facts, because it is too big of a price to get to the root of the problem.*

Although such a couple may have sex, the intimacy is long gone. The lips stop communicating, then they stop kissing. The lack of kissing says, "You have betrayed me, and I don't trust you anymore." This, again, is the end result of passivity—letting communication break down and not assertively expressing needs, but suppressing true feelings. Slowly, resentment builds up, feelings shut down and true intimacy is not experienced—although the couple may go through all the actions of marriage.

87

Many good men are notorious for behavior such as forcing their wives to make all the decisions, refusing to take an active role in the children's lives and letting their wives take all spiritual leadership in the family. Not every woman who does so has a Jezebel-like personality. Most women with passive husbands resent this behavior because they have a God-given desire to follow a husband's leadership and they are not comfortable making all the decisions. Sometimes such wives are accused of being Jezebels, when the truth is that they have married a passive man who has handed over his God-given role as spiritual head, leader and teacher. These wives have been forced to accept the authority handed to them from a passive husband.

Healing begins in dysfunctional marriages when one spouse calls the other to wholeness, saying, "Please stop doing this and start doing that." When this is done in an assertive way, it brings the other partner back. As intimacy begins anew, both partners know they are becoming more whole through behavioral changes.

Gone with the Wind

You are probably familiar with the classic movie *Gone with the Wind*. Scarlett O'Hara was the aggressive personality totally consumed with herself and her own needs. Rhett Butler was the pursuer in the relationship, while she was avoidant. However, he could be labeled as passive because he bent over backward trying to please her, relentlessly trying to get her to love him. Ultimately, he came to the place of giving up and truly meaning it when he told her, "Frankly, my dear . . ." He loved her, but also loved himself enough not to take any more abuse.

This happens in the Jezebel-Ahab relationships where the passive person finally says, "Enough!" As often happens in such relationships, when Scarlett finally "came around" and desired to work on the relationship, Rhett had emotionally shut down and could not open himself up to her. Sadly, often this is the outcome. Instead of seeing the truth that he had finally gotten what he wanted and she was finally available to be intimate, he shut down and sabotaged the intimacy by being unwilling to forgive. Rhett Butler encountered the saboteur within.

This is so true in passive relationships. Passive people reach a point where they finally stop trying to get the avoidant partner to love them. They are ready to move on with their lives, but it is too late for the avoidant ones who are finally realizing what they are losing. The passive person has shut down and emotionally does not feel anything anymore. In fact, even in a situation where the passive person does decide to get back into the relationship, it should only be when the avoidant partner has done his or her own soul searching and has gotten healing.

Ahab and Jezebel personalities can harm or destroy more than just marriages, though. Next we will look at how these personalities play out in other real-life relationships.

7

Lifetime Patterns

Angie experienced a difficult childhood. She grew up in an extremely dysfunctional family. She remembers distinctly a time when she was only five years old and her grandfather fondled her chest. Her grandmother walked out of the bathroom and witnessed the entire thing. Minutes later, she called Angie over and said, "Don't ever let him do that to you again."

Can you imagine telling that to a five year old, as if it is her fault? Her grandmother could have rebuked her grandfather or even told Angie's dad, but she put the guilt on her little granddaughter. Because of this grandmother's behavior, Angie carried a wound into later life that affected her deeply. What pain could have been avoided if the grandmother had confronted the perpetrator and reassured Angie that this was not her fault! But her grandmother took the easy way out by not confronting the other adult and by putting the responsibility on a young child instead—doing irreparable damage in the process.

Unquestionably, our behavior patterns begin with events early in our lives. So often, one person could make a significant difference by showing some concern in the life of a victim. Unfortunately, people who live for years and years with a passive nature decide to let things slide. This creates lifetime patterns of harm, depression and even heartbreaking circumstances in relationships of all kinds.

A Tragedy of Passivity

Linda was an innocent girl of nine when her eighteen-year-old uncle maliciously planned to get her alone one afternoon and rape her. What makes it more sickening is that her uncle was newly married and had planned this outing with his niece, telling his wife and Linda's parents that the two of them would be on an adventure together. Her father and mother did not recognize the uncle's evil motives. He took Linda to his apartment and robbed her of her virginity. In the following years, the uncle included his two brothers in the conquest, and all three regularly had intercourse with her until she was sixteen.

Linda surrendered to passivity because the abuse started when she was so young and she did not know how to make it stop. She eventually married and had three children, but she battled extreme depression for years. Finally she admitted herself into a psychiatric hospital for treatment. However, working toward wholeness seemed like a double-edged sword to her. She was afraid of being depressed and suicidal, but she was also afraid to live. While in the hospital, she told her sister one night, "I've lived my life depressed for so long, I don't know how to live it any other way." The next day, Linda committed suicide.

Following the funeral, family members found her journal that detailed the abuse she had suffered at the hands of various family members. Her brothers and sisters confronted the uncles, but only one of the three admitted that it was all true. The one who first raped her denied everything. Linda also wrote in the journal about her grandfather, who had prided himself on always washing his hands before eating. He even criticized others for not doing the same, yet he sexually molested numerous female family members. Linda pointed out the irony that although he was a child molester, at least he washed his hands before every meal. It reminds me of how Jesus exposed the hypocrisy of the Pharisees: "Woe to you, scribes and Pharisees, hypocrites! For you cleanse the outside of the cup and dish, but inside they are full of extortion and self-indulgence" (Matthew 23:25).

After her death, Linda's bereaved family read her fantasy story about a little girl who was loved and protected by her parents. Sadly, young Linda's passive mother was divorced and highly involved with her own boyfriends. She either did not notice Linda's pain or chose to look the other way. Her father, although a good provider, was always emotionally uninvolved in the family and therefore blind to Linda's needs. How Linda had longed for protection, but she had no one to come to her rescue.

Like Mother, Like Daughter

Meredith's dream was to attend art school, yet at the age of eighteen she was pregnant and unmarried. Her boyfriend had just finished a jail sentence for involvement in drugs and did not show much interest in working. How did Meredith get to this place?

Meredith learned passivity from her mother. When Meredith was eleven years old, her stepfather molested her. When her mother found out, she immediately took the children and left. However, she later returned to the man, causing Meredith to feel unloved, unprotected and insecure. When Meredith turned seventeen, her mother allowed her to have her boyfriend live in the house with them. How different her life might have been if her mother had been strong and assertive and protected her at the age of eleven instead of trying to make it up to her by being too permissive when Meredith was a teenager.

How many times do we hear the familiar story of a young teenage girl sleeping with her boyfriend? Without the love and attention of a caring father, that daughter is looking for someone to tell her she is valued and worthy of love. If the father has been absent in the relationship, he has passed up an opportunity to prevent a multitude of problems. The best thing any father can do is continually affirm his daughters from an early age and not passively hope they will turn out okay.

Avoiding Confrontation

Dennis died young of cancer, leaving three sons. While he was a brilliant person, he did not appear able to relate either as a husband or, later, as a father. He was perfectionistic and controlling, and he held everyone hostage in fear of his temper and moods. His wife, Marie, was a true Pollyanna who constantly denied her own feelings and did not call on her husband to get help for his issues. She usually felt responsible for his anger and sugarcoated the difficulties.

After Dennis's untimely death, two of the boys blamed their mother for their not having a better relationship with their father. The boys blamed her because she had not called their dad to grow up emotionally and spiritually and be a husband and a father. The third and youngest son vowed never to be like his father and felt it was his responsibility to defend his mother to his older brothers.

All three sons have spiritual and emotional issues that Marie now recognizes could have been avoided had she not passively looked the other way in her marriage.

Adult Children and Parents

At 22, Susan was a young, beautiful graduate of an Ivy League school. During college, she had become involved with Greg, who was 24. After three years of an intimate relationship with him and a year of engagement, she found out that Greg was also dating another woman. Susan ended their engagement, but not before she took some time to work through the situation and find out how she could move on toward health and wholeness.

During their time together, Susan had done everything she could to please Greg, even allowing him to use her financially. He also emotionally degraded her on numerous occasions, both privately and in front of her parents. His out-of-line behaviors went unchallenged until Susan finally drew the line with his infidelity. She agonized about leaving him, and the dilemma of whether or not to do so involved her parents and friends. She was torn between their opinions and what she felt her heart was telling her to do. Codependent, Susan was driven by what everyone else thought (particularly her mother), yet her feelings were telling her that he was her life mate. Through counseling, she was able to see the obviously abusive situation for what it was, and she knew she must take a close look at the relationship and what she could learn from it.

She finally decided to begin counseling sessions with Greg. On the advice of her therapist, she asked her parents to join her in her individual session. As often happens in therapy, Susan apprehensively entered the session with her parents and stated that she had worried about the appointment all day. Susan was positioned in a chair across from her parents, who sat on a couch. They seemed ready to listen to her and did not verbally agree or disagree on the subject of her boyfriend, with whom Susan had been trying to reconnect.

The object of this session was to help Susan differentiate from her parents, who had up to this time played a very controlling, yet loving role in her life. Her parents listened to her primarily because they had agreed to do so to help her, even though their opinion was the polar opposite of hers. They felt Greg was neither emotionally nor financially stable enough to be a husband and simply was not husband material.

Apprehensively, Susan began speaking to her mother about her issues with her as a parent. Her father listened and appeared interested in her mother's demeanor, which was very attentive—until she broke out of the dialogue and asked the therapist if what Susan found painful and hurtful about her parents was not, in fact, just normal. Susan's mother could not even recognize the degree of her control. Her father had always had her mother on a pedestal and had always let her control Susan completely. Susan reacted to this later by partnering with someone who wanted to be on a pedestal, too—Greg. She had followed the relationship pattern of her father with her mother.

The breakthrough for Susan came later in the session, as her parents continued to listen to and validate what their daughter was saying. Susan began to feel like more of an adult around her parents. She also saw how her behavior with Greg had been strikingly similar to the way she had coped with her parents—never questioning them, always trying to please them. She recognized that her passivity with her boyfriend had begun out of a childhood in which her parents were very loving but very controlling, giving little attention to her actual needs.

Susan also saw that her father had done everything for her mother and that she herself was headed for a life of doing everything for her potential husband—someone who wanted her to take care of him. Greg did not want to move into being the leader of the relationship—a God-given position. He also did not want to take responsibility for himself.

Once Susan made these discoveries and connections, she decided she wanted to permanently end her relationship with

Greg. This was a healthy decision. She should have broken it off much sooner because of Greg's emotional, physical and spiritual abuse. However, Greg's infidelity happened to be the deal breaker for her. People often either stay in or leave relationships for the wrong reasons.

Siblings without Communication

Crystal was born the middle girl of five sisters. Sadly, her mother was a controlling Jezebel and at times was jealous even of her own daughters. She often refused to allow Crystal and her two older sisters to sit on their father's lap or enjoy his love and affection. Their father was very passive, always cowering to their mother even at the cost of not being free to express love to his own children.

As a result of their parents' dynamics, the girls grew up in harsh patterns of communication with one another. Theirs had been an outwardly religious home filled with more condemnation and guilt than love and acceptance, until they were not free to express themselves and be who they were. Crystal was the classic people pleaser and would allow herself to be drawn into constant conflicts with her sisters. She related how she and one sister would gossip about another on one day, then a different sister would judge the others another day. They all silently competed with each other in marriages, children, homes, friends and even church activities.

Crystal ultimately reached a point where she divorced herself from any relationship with her sisters. At one point all the dysfunction had blown up in their faces, and all five sisters had come clean about what they had said about each other. The damage was massive, and the end result was that all ties between the sisters were severed. This family loved the Lord, but they had allowed passivity to run rampant and steal healthy family ties.

Passive Pastors

In ministry, every leader has to deal with the impossibility of trying to make everyone happy. If he is passive, he will live in fear of not pleasing people and often compromise his message in order to avoid offending anyone. A friend of mine who pastors a growing church was approached several years ago by a member who was a prosperous businessman and a significant tither. The Holy Spirit had begun to move in the church in a powerful way, but this was not suitable to this member, so he asked for a meeting with the pastor.

On the way to the meeting, the Lord spoke to the pastor, telling him the man was unhappy. The Lord said, *If you make him promises, you will be able to keep him, but he will become your source instead of Me.*

When they sat down to talk, the man asked his pastor, "Aren't you afraid of leading God's people astray?"

The pastor answered, "I'm more afraid of taking God's people nowhere."

At that, the man let the pastor know that he did not approve of the way the Spirit was "moving" in the church, and he got up and left, soon joining another church.

Passive pastors struggle with standing up to people who have a controlling spirit. Usually there is a high price to pay for confrontation because these controllers are well networked in the congregation and will do much damage. Many passive leaders have cowered in fear, never confronting Jezebel behavior and looking the other way instead. Needless to say, the work of the Holy Spirit is then hindered.

Many churches have died spiritually (although they may appear outwardly prosperous) because a passive leader was never able to take a stand to please the Holy Spirit more than people. At some point, every leader has to make a choice between being a man pleaser or a God pleaser. The fear of man is a snare.

The Good Side of Confrontation

Bill always longed for acknowledgment. So when Mike, a co-worker, befriended him, he was happy—until he saw that Mike was always trying to get him to join in criticizing and judging another co-worker. This scenario occurred on numerous occasions before Bill recognized it for what it was, a pattern of behavior he allowed because he so desperately wanted acceptance. He had a mild personality, but he was finally able to draw a line and say to Mike, "I'm not okay with talking about this person unless he is here with us. So unless he is here, I have to say that I don't have a dog in that fight."

Because Bill was a Christian, he knew the principle that Jesus taught, that it was not right to talk about this other co-worker without addressing him personally. "Moreover if your brother sins against you, go and tell him his fault between you and him alone" (Matthew 18:15). Bill finally confronted his own passive behavior and put a stop to it.

What happens to those who never take responsibility and confront their issues? Those who visit the elderly in convalescent homes have witnessed the behavior of those who have repressed their feelings all their lives. Now, at the age where they are no longer mentally capable of suppressing their emotions, they are often angry and speak with nasty attitudes. At the end of their lives, when their ability to inhibit their responses is gone, everything held inside for so long comes to the surface.

At the end of our lives, we will still hold inside whatever we have repressed. What we do not deal with now, we will have to deal with even as we die. By not dealing with issues of passivity during our lifetime, we are sowing pain and sadness into our hearts.

One wonderful example of just the opposite was a woman who for a long time had attended a church where a friend of mine was the pastor. She ultimately was diagnosed with

Alzheimer's, but since she had always dealt with issues head-on during her life, her disposition at the end of her life stayed sweet. Just weeks before she was placed in a nursing home, she showed up at church on the wrong day. Her mind, though confused, was telling her to go to church. There was nothing in her heart but her focus on going to church!

Confronting ourselves or others when necessary has a good side. It is to the glory of God when we choose to deal with issues assertively and to live with self-respect, consistently drawing healthy boundaries for ourselves and our relationships. I am so saddened when I observe people who have Ahab-like issues of pride, denial, projection and so on, yet they go into eternity claiming to be the victim all the way to the end—still bitter, still angry, still in denial.

There is no need to come to the end of our lives with unresolved issues. God has made provision through His Son so that we can live an abundant life (see John 10:10) and grow up into mature people, whole and healed, coming into "the knowledge of the Son of God, to a perfect man, to the measure of the stature of the fullness of Christ" (Ephesians 4:13).

Next we will look at defense mechanisms that create behavior patterns in our relationships. Only when we stop ourselves from employing these mechanisms can we learn to avoid returning to our old patterns of passivity.

8

Defense Mechanisms

Defense mechanisms are best defined as tools we create to protect ourselves. We use them to cope and to help us maintain a feeling of security. Depending on where traumatic events in our lives fall on a continuum of minor to severe, they can lead us into different coping behaviors, not all of which are done on a conscious level. The defense mechanisms that follow are examples of passive behavior, though some of them can show up in Jezebel-like personalities, too. They are all distortions of reality that we use to suppress anxiety or tension.

Remember, when we have an Ahab spirit of passivity or a Jezebel spirit of aggressiveness, we can easily slip into defense mode. However, when we recognize our tendency to put up these defenses, we can ask God to help us transform our unhealthy behaviors into more positive, healthy and assertive ways of living.

As you look at your own relationships and determine not to live passively, watch out for these behavioral patterns. Ask yourself the questions that the following list contains. Conflict and tension inevitably will tempt you to resort to some of these defense mechanisms, but remember where the old, familiar ways of dealing with conflict got you—trapped in passivity. It is time to break free of them.

Denial: A refusal to believe or accept reality, blocking it out and behaving as if circumstances or painful events do not exist.

The defense mechanism of denial sometimes begins with a traumatic event in early childhood that is too painful to face. A child is not well equipped to process a severely traumatic event, so he or she suppresses it as if it never happened. Subconsciously the child (who is now an adult) believes that if the event is acknowledged as the truth of what really happened, then he or she will have to deal with it—so it is easier to repress it, avoid change and not deal with it.

Questions to ask: Am I unwilling to look at reality? Am I pretending something does not exist in order to avoid pain?

Projection: Attributing something disturbing in our lives to someone else.

This mechanism can often show up in aggressive as well as passive behavior. Rather than face an issue of pride, for example, it is easier to accuse another person of the pride we are acting out. The reason we project—consciously or subconsciously—is that sometimes we do not recognize our own dysfunction. So rather than changing, we just accuse other people of the behaviors we are exhibiting.

For example, Brian's girlfriend made a scene in a restaurant because their order was taking too long. Later in the car, she accused him of causing a scene, but he had not said one word during the exchange! In another case, years ago my friend had moved into a new apartment and overheard a couple talking. The woman was crying because her husband had beaten her. Unbelievably, the man said to his crying wife, "Why do you make me do that?" He probably had seen his father abuse his mother and then blame her, and he was repeating the familiar behavior. He projected the blame onto his wife, seeing his actions as her fault.

Projection is the age-old problem of refusing to take responsibility—not taking the plank out of our own eye first, and instead seeing the speck in the other person's eye (see Matthew 7:5). Projection can be convenient for passive people because they can shift behaviors onto aggressive people around them who are far more demonstrative in their behavior. Passivity is much more covert, while aggression is much more overt.

Question to ask: Do I attribute my own disturbing impulses, behaviors and traits to someone else?

Repression: A voluntary or involuntary removal of something from the conscious mind, pushing it down inside as if it never happened, although the person still may have knowledge of it.

Soon after experiencing the traumatic birth of her first child, Phyllis also experienced painful memories of childhood sexual abuse that were surfacing for the first time. The trauma of birth seemed to put her in touch with those old traumatic events.

People who have been sexually abused often repress the painful memories. The events are so painful to remember that they are buried indefinitely. This type of passivity can turn aggressive, with the abused person taking the stance, "I'm not going to be hurt again."

Questions to ask: Is part of my problem that I avoid dealing with repressed memories I have not processed? Am I allowing the unfinished business of repressed memories to control my life and influence the choices I make today?

Displacement: The expression of any repressed feeling transferred toward a person, place or thing other than the actual source (usually toxic), such as taking anger out on a pet.

103

One man told me that his wife would never talk to him about what was upsetting her. Instead, she would bring up an irrelevant subject, stirring up strife and negative emotions all as a "cover" so the real issue would not be discussed.

Another example comes from a couple who were both in their second marriage. One day federal agents visited the man at work and said that his son was involved in drug trafficking. When the man came home, to his wife's surprise he went into a tirade about some insignificant behavior shown by her son from another marriage.

Displacement behavior serves to distract oneself and/or others (intentionally or unintentionally) from having to deal with the issue at hand. It becomes easier to magnify an issue that does not even relate to the current problem.

Questions to ask: Am I guilty of dodging issues? Of not taking responsibility to deal with a specific problem, transferring blame to someone or something else instead?

Reaction Formation: Repressing an impulse and replacing it with the opposite behavior in an exaggerated way.

A spouse might inwardly say or make the subconscious vow, *What you've done really ticks me off, so I'm going to be overly nice to you. I'm going to kill you with kindness, although I hate your guts.* The bottom line is that the person is passive toward the real underlying issue.

Questions to ask: Do I avoid telling others about what I need and want by passively putting up with more of their poor behavior? Do I change my behavior to disguise my real feelings?

Rationalization: Using false logic to explain behavior.

Examples of rationalization would be "I'm already overweight, so I'll eat anything," or "You've already accused me of running around, so I'll just go ahead and do it." Again, this kind of passivity says that we are not facing the underlying issues.

Questions to ask: Do I mistake irrational, unacceptable behavior for logical behavior and learn to live with it? Do I often blame others instead of accepting responsibility for my actions?

Intellectualization: Depriving an experience of feelings, although it has come to the consciousness, because the event was so difficult that it is the only way a person can handle it.

In intellectualization, we refuse to wrap our feelings around the reality of an event. Instead, we look at it logically and remove the emotions to avoid experiencing their pain. For example, a wife knows her husband has a mistress, but reasons that maybe the mistress is meeting a need she cannot meet for him. The wife therefore intellectualizes his behavior as logical and refuses to experience the painful emotion of rejection.

Question to ask: Do I separate my feelings from a situation, thinking of all possible angles but never taking action—just analyzing, reasoning and justifying?

Undoing: Doing something unacceptable and then doing something else to try to make up for the wounds.

For example, a man abuses his wife and then does something really nice for her, like buying flowers. He is trying to undo the hurt by putting a little bandage on a huge wound. This is passivity because he does not face his wrong behavior; he buys her flowers merely as an act designed to make himself feel better.

Another example is a woman's husband who would not let her follow her dream of starting her own court-reporting business because he was such a controlling Jezebel and did not want her to be out in the world doing business with men. After he forbade her to start the business, he bought her some diamond jewelry. Sadly, she sold out to him and traded her lifelong dream for some diamond jewelry. Obviously, his behavior was aggressive and strongly manipulative, but her behavior was passive—giving up her dream and not respecting herself.

Questions to ask: Do I excuse my bad behavior by doing something else in exchange? Do I substitute "feel-good" actions so I can feel better about my behavior instead of facing the truth and repenting? Am I putting a band-aid on my behavior?

Minimizing: Reducing the importance of an issue in order to balance out a partner's reaction.

A husband beats his wife, but she tells herself that he did not really mean it; that he has been under stress. She may even blame herself, saying, "I shouldn't have said what I said." Some wives make excuses for an alcoholic husband—"He hasn't been drinking as much lately"—instead of requiring him to take responsibility. This minimizes the effect of the harm he has done and lets him off the hook. This is classic passivity, taking no action instead of calling the person to a place of responsibility and defining appropriate boundaries.

Questions to ask: Am I quick to make excuses for those who have abused me? Am I afraid to assertively confront those who have crossed boundaries, not calling them to take responsibility for their actions?

Maximizing/Catastrophizing: Making an issue larger than it is in order to balance out someone else's lack of emotional response.

This involves dramatization, displacing or guilt. It is always making more out of a situation than is accurate. A wife is starved emotionally and asks her husband for some space in order to find some healing, so the husband begins to monitor every detail of his wife's actions, as if she were planning to leave him.

Questions to ask: Do I expect disaster? Is everything a catastrophe? Do I hear about a problem and start with "what-ifs?" "What if tragedy strikes?" "What if it happens to me?"

Compartmentalization: Acting with two sets of value systems when part of the self is separated from an awareness of other parts of the self.

A good example of this defense mechanism is someone who projects a good Christian image in public, but in private is abusive to his wife and kids or is involved in pornography. Or someone who coaches Little League but behind closed doors is a child molester. Or high-powered professionals who are highly respected in the community, who then go home to their families and are very abusive.

Questions to ask: Do I live with two sets of value systems? Am I guilty of living one life in public and another in private?

Blaming: Blaming someone else for anything one does not want to take responsibility for; sometimes blaming oneself unnecessarily.

To avoid bringing any negative attention to or disapproval on ourselves, we may use this defense mechanism to place blame on someone else. If we take responsibility for poor behavior, then we have to change or make it right, and that is too hard. This avoidance technique does not necessarily stem from the conscious mind. This is vintage Jezebel behavior. Jezebels rarely take responsibility—it is always someone else's fault.

Sometimes people will also blame themselves for something of which they are not guilty—such as berating themselves for knocking over a glass of water.

Questions to ask: Do I hold other people responsible for my pain? Do I blame myself for problems, calling myself a failure and an idiot?

Overspiritualizing: Transferring everything to God.

Here a person never takes personal responsibility because they claim God told them to do or not to do something. I have encountered so many instances of this in which a person would not receive correction or constructive criticism because they seemed to separate reality from the truth. Because of perceived rejection, they avoid dealing with conflicts, then they blame their inactivity and passivity about things on God or the devil.

Questions to ask: Do I avoid dealing with the truth by overspiritualizing an issue? Do I put things off and then blame God or the devil when I have not taken responsibility for something appropriately?

Dramatization: Drawing attention to oneself because of an addiction to drama.

Overly dramatic individuals do not know how to get their needs met in a healthy, honest and assertive way. If no chaos is going on, they create chaos, usually to get attention. Even if chaos brings negative attention, it is still attention!

This mechanism is probably best described as passive-aggressive. A child might carry on with a fit, knowing the parents will give in just so they do not have to listen to it. In another scenario, a friend of mine was in a relationship with a very needy girlfriend. If he did not call her at a certain time or forgot to compliment her on something, she would immediately dramatize the situation, which would then escalate to unbelievable emotional tension. This would put her in control, and she would "earn" the attention she was craving. He would act too passively, trying to keep the peace rather than refusing to let her embellish the situation.

Questions to ask: Do I use an offense or a quandary to overdramatize my feelings? Do I involve others by drawing them into a scenario of turmoil that does not even exist?

Filtering: A victim mentality in which everything that is said is fed into a negative mindset, reinforcing a person's subconscious belief that he or she is always the victim.

This filtering mechanism always gives power away. A woman told me about her brother, who perceived that she had yelled at him when she had simply told him the blunt truth about something. Even though she apologized, he went away and repeated the "incident" to everyone. If he had been assertive and accepted her apology, then he could no longer have felt like the victim. But he had to skew the real details of their verbal exchange through his negative mental filter so he could continue to be the victim. His problem was that he always had to be in the right and put everyone else in the wrong so he could look like the victim.

The root of filtering is that a person is so afraid of rejection on any level that he or she cannot handle facing issues as they really are.

Question to ask: Am I filtering conversations and reactions through a belief system that maintains that I am a victim?

Escapism: Letting life revolve around things that do not really matter in the long run.

In defending oneself through escapism, a person lives with issues in the background that he or she chooses not to deal with—so it is important to always keep busy with endless, mindless tasks to avoid facing the difficult things.

People might become workaholics and bury themselves in a career, job or activity, all to escape a brutal confrontation with that part of life or relationships they cannot face. They often seek comfort in counterfeit affections, addictions, compulsions, busyness and hyperreligious activity.

Questions to ask: Do I let myself become preoccupied with behavior that causes me to avoid confronting real problems in my relationships? Have I become consumed with something in life that causes me to escape my real issues?

People Pleasing: Living life with an exaggerated need to make everyone else happy.

People pleasers live like chameleons—always changing in order to get what they want without being detected as manipulators. They do their best to conform to their environments and keep everyone else happy. They often overextend themselves to an extreme of sacrifice and self-denial, then resent it.

Questions to ask: Am I constantly changing myself or my plans so I can be accepted? Am I giving with expectations and becoming resentful when they are not met? Am I a chameleon—always conforming to my environment?

Polarized Thinking: Swinging from one end of a continuum to the other in regard to how one thinks and feels about a person, place or thing.

Polarized thinking sometimes affects people's views of God. They often think that they are in good with God at times, but if they screw up, He will reject them. A healthy perspective would be, "I've had a bad day, but God still loves me—who I am is not defined by my past or my circumstances. What I've done is not who I am. I am a human being and not a human doing. I am made in God's image and called to His likeness."

Questions to ask: Am I either on top of the world or in a pit? Do things have to be black and white, good or bad? Do I have to be perfect or a failure—perceiving that there is no middle ground? Am I learning to forgive myself and give myself grace?

Overgeneralization: Making judgments about others based on too little information.

For instance, if you saw someone eat junk food once, then you assume the person always eats it. Or if you saw someone drink one glass of wine, then you assume he or she is an alcoholic.

Questions to ask: Do I make broad assumptions based on a single conversation or a single observation? Do I judge people based on their reactions without knowing all the facts?

Mind Reading: Expecting others to recognize one's needs, or making judgments and assumptions about other people's hearts and motives.

Mind readers assume they know what other people are feeling or why they act the way they do.

Questions to ask: Do I assume that I know how people are feeling toward me? Am I angry when people do not read my mind and fulfill my expectations of them?

Personalization: A personal exaltation of oneself as having more power or less power than what is factual. Comparing oneself to others to determine who is smarter, better looking, etc.

Questions to ask: Do I think everything people do or everything they say is some kind of reaction to me? Do I downplay others and criticize them, attempting to exalt myself to a better position?

Shoulds: Having a personal standard of do's and don'ts concerning people's behavior.

This is highly toxic, coming out of a very wounded place, and involves unrealistic expectations for oneself or others. One example could be having thoughts such as *I should have been there to rescue that person*, or *They should have been there to rescue me* when it would have been impossible.

Questions to ask: Do I have a list of ironclad rules about how other people (or I) should act—my own secret standards? Do people who break my rules anger me? Do I feel guilty if I break the rules?

Emotional Reasoning: Living from an emotional perspective in every situation. Allowing feelings to determine the truth versus allowing the truth to determine feelings.

Questions to ask: Do I believe that what I feel automatically must be true? If I feel stupid and boring, then do I believe I must *be* stupid and boring?

Passivity: Giving power away, not taking responsibility for one's own life or for getting one's emotional needs met.

111

This involves offering little or no resistance to unfair treatment and nursing resentment because needs are not met in a healthy way.

Questions to ask: Am I stuffing my emotions? Am I being a peacekeeper, keeping peace at any price? Do I fear confrontations and/or rejection?

Aggression: Taking power away from others; not respecting people's personal boundaries.

Questions to ask: Am I being controlling? Am I being pushy to get what I want? Is my agenda "Get them before they get me"?

Dropping Our Defenses

Do you see yourself as a participant in any of the above behaviors? In your responses to conflict, have you recognized any of these traits coming to the surface? It is much easier to use one of these defense mechanisms than to confront our issues. Yet when we persist in putting up defense mechanisms, we rob ourselves of the opportunity to find our real identity (made in God's image)—as opposed to living in a false identity (man's image and how we think people view us).

If we overuse defense mechanisms, we stay stuck in our dysfunction and do not experience the freedom and abundant life that Jesus already purchased for us. We must drop our defenses and allow Him to transform us from the inside out. The Holy Spirit is the Spirit of truth, and listening to Him will set us free, however painful it may be to face our issues.

In the next chapter, we will look at how continuing in our passivity ultimately robs us of our identity. However, we will also see that like King David, we can ward off identity theft and reclaim our identity as children of God.

9

Identity Theft

My friend Jeff is a kind and outgoing person, but he never seems to be able to accept himself. As long as I have known Jeff, he has prominently displayed photos of himself taken with this or that celebrity whom he met on some occasion. Any time I stop by his home, Jeff immediately points out his latest photo and tells me the whole story of a conversation he has had with a certain celebrity or how well he knows one of them.

As Jeff's friend, I totally accept him for who he is. Yet it is obvious that he cannot accept himself unless he connects himself to people that he sees as famous or important. Jeff obviously struggles with his own identity—he only feels significant during his brief interludes with well-known people.

I have another friend whose identity seems tied up in his possessions. Keith is always in pursuit of owning more and more things. Whether it is the newest technological gadget, an antique car, a new car or a fancier house, nothing seems to satisfy his insatiable desire for more. It seems obvious to me that Keith also struggles with his identity. He seems to feel good about himself only when he is surrounded with material things. His identity has been stolen, and his worth is tied to the value of his possessions.

One of the most common and dreaded crimes today is identity theft. Con artists continually attempt to find enough of your personal information to steal your identity. Many victims of identity theft have spent many years and thousands of dollars to clear their names and get their credit and reputations restored. A commercial for one company that claims to help people avoid identity theft declares that an identity is stolen every three seconds.

What does identity theft have to do with an Ahab-like spirit of passivity? Everything! Passivity involves far more than a personality trait or a difficult set of relationships. In battling passivity, we are battling a spiritual enemy! Tragically, the enemy has successfully lied to believers in order to rob them of their two "I's." He wants to steal their *identity* and stop their *influence*.

Many of us who struggle with our identity have accepted Satan's lies about ourselves and have become passive. We have given up our power, authority and influence. Capitulating to the Ahab spirit, we have fallen for the devil's strategy of convincing us to not feel good about ourselves. The enemy's lies leave us craving acceptance and living life more to please others than to please God.

Who Are You?

Most people do not know they are victims of identity theft. Do you know if you are?

You might say:

- "I'm an engineer." But that is not who you are. That is your occupation and training.

114

- "I live in Texas." But that is not who you are. That is where you live.
- "I am married to ____." But that is not who you are. That is your spouse.
- "I have a master's degree and a doctorate." But that is not who you are. That just represents goals you have achieved.
- "I live in a beautiful, 4,000-square-foot house with a swimming pool in the back." But that is not who you are. That just represents some success you have enjoyed.
- "I drive a fast convertible." But that is not who you are. That is just a possession.
- "I go to this wonderful church." But that is not who you are. That is where you worship God and fellowship with other believers.
- "I'm a father/mother, a son/daughter, a grandfather/grandmother, an aunt/uncle." But that is not who you are. That is a role you have in this earthly life.

Who are you, then? *You are a son or daughter of God*—truly made in God's image at the moment of conception. You have great value because Jesus Christ, who knew no sin, was crucified for your sins and endowed you with constant access to the Holy Spirit, who is here with you forever (see 2 Corinthians 5:21). This is the greatest revelation and awakening you will ever have.

Too many have "found" their identity in something they have accomplished, in someone they know, in somewhere they live, in some skill they possess, in some family trait or in some possession. But none of these areas should define our lives. Only God can define us, and He has chosen to define us as His sons and daughters. We should represent Him on this earth.

If you are a woman, it does not matter how feminine you are—you are a son of God. If you are a man, it does not matter how macho or masculine you feel—you are the Bride of Christ. If you struggle with your identity in Christ, you cannot fully grasp the power of God. But when you know who you are, the forces of darkness are in trouble!

It is vital to know who God has created *you* to be. For too long, believers have resorted to imitating other Christians they see doing things for God. But by emulating others, they compromise their own identities simply to become clones of someone they have seen God work through in some way. Many great men and women of God have not only been followed and eulogized, but they also have been imitated by those hoping to acquire similar results. Certainly nothing is wrong with appreciating the way God uses another person, but to imitate someone else misses the point. Following a formula or admiring the success of another believer is no substitute for establishing your own identity in Christ. *Everyone is born an original, but sadly, most people die a copy.*

For each one of us, nothing can compare to finding our own niche and function in the Body of Christ. We are each a designer original!

Does Satan Fear You?

Those caught in the bondage of passivity are unable or un-willing to exercise their authority as children of God. As a result, they are of little threat to the powers of darkness. Paul said:

> For we do not wrestle against flesh and blood, but against principalities [not personalities], against powers, against the rulers of the darkness of this age, against spiritual hosts of wickedness in the heavenly places.
>
> Ephesians 6:12

Recently, a friend invited me to go horseback riding with a group of people. I readily agreed, thinking it would be fun.

While I had grown up on a farm, it had been many years since I had ridden a horse. As the owner was saddling up the horses, I began to feel nervous, recognizing their massive strength and energy. The owner said, "Steve, I'm going to have you ride this horse because he's more mature and comfortable being ridden."

As soon as I mounted the horse, however, I knew I was in trouble. I felt very insecure, and I could not find the on-and-off switch. I could tell the horse sensed my trepidation and lack of confidence. I was sure he was thinking, *I'm going to have fun with this guy.* I started off following behind three other riders for about twenty minutes. Then, without warning, my horse decided to lie down. Then it tried to roll over on me! I yelled for help and was quickly rescued, trading my horse for an even older one. But I will never forget that day. The horse sensed my fear and seemed to say, "You don't know who you are!"

I think the same scenario is true when we Christians try to exercise our faith and take authority over the devil. Many times, we are not yet convinced of the position and authority we have in Christ.

This seems true when we read about what happened in the city of Ephesus. Paul had been ministering there for months, and great miracles were being accomplished:

> God worked unusual miracles by the hands of Paul, so that even handkerchiefs or aprons were brought from his body to the sick, and the diseases left them and the evil spirits went out of them.
>
> Acts 19:11–12

But one day, some Jewish exorcists began trying some of this supernatural ministry. However, they did not have their identity in a relationship with God, so they simply tried to imitate what they saw the apostles doing. The results were disastrous:

117

> Then some of the itinerant Jewish exorcists took it upon themselves to call the name of the Lord Jesus over those who had evil spirits, saying, "We exorcise you by the Jesus whom Paul preaches." Also there were seven sons of Sceva, a Jewish chief priest, who did so.
>
> And the evil spirit answered and said, "Jesus I know, and Paul I know, but who are you?"
>
> Then the man in whom the evil spirit was leaped on them, overpowered them, and prevailed against them, so that they fled out of that house naked and wounded.
>
> Acts 19:13–16

The evil spirit recognized that these seven men did not have an identity in Christ. They could only offer a hollow imitation.

The enemy certainly is not threatened if we only imitate someone else's experience of taking authority in Christ. There is no substitute for having our own identity in Christ and an intimate relationship with the Holy Spirit.

We Are God's Instruments

We passive people rarely feel God can use us. We think we just are not qualified enough. We believe everyone else is more spiritual than we are. However, God wants to use us as His instruments in daily situations. As we recognize who we are in Christ and realize the authority He gives us as believers, we will encounter more and more divine appointments.

This is just what happened to Peter and John. Shortly after the resurrection of Jesus, Peter and John went to the Temple to pray. As they proceeded toward the Temple at nine o'clock that morning, they passed a familiar sight:

> A certain man lame from his mother's womb was carried, whom they laid daily at the gate of the temple which is called Beautiful, to ask alms from those who entered the temple.
>
> Acts 3:2

This man was carried to the same spot outside the Temple each day to capitalize on the compassion and sympathy of those entering it to pray. Jesus Himself must have passed this man hundreds of times. I wonder if the disciples questioned why Jesus never healed this man?

But that morning was different, and I am sure it caught Peter and John by surprise! That morning, the Holy Spirit obviously had a special purpose in mind. The man, "seeing Peter and John about to go into the temple, asked for alms," a familiar request (verse 3). But Peter and John were under the mandate of the Holy Spirit. They must have encountered the presence of God and an awareness that something wonderful was about to happen: "Fixing his eyes on him, with John, Peter said, 'Look at us'" (verse 4).

Notice what the apostles did not say. They did not say, "Look to Jesus." They did not say, "Come to our great church!" They did not say, "We have a great pastor." They did not say, "We'll go on a fast for you." Peter and John knew their identity in Christ—Himself. They recognized they were sons of God and that He was their identity. Therefore, they could boldly say, "Look at us!"

When we understand that we are children of God and that the Holy Spirit in us gives us the power to affect anyone in our path, our lives are forever changed. Heaven applauds! We know our identity. Many believers do not know who they are and still pray with a question mark instead of with godly authority and confidence.

The second thing Peter and John said to the lame man also had great significance. Peter said, "Silver and gold I do not have, but what I do have I give you: In the name of Jesus Christ of Nazareth, rise up and walk" (verse 6). Then the man—who was crippled from birth and had never walked—not only was healed, but he went walking and leaping and praising God. Peter "took him by the right hand and lifted him up, and immediately his feet and ankle bones received strength. So he, leaping up, stood and walked and entered the temple with them—walking, leaping, and praising God" (verses 7–8).

Peter said, "What I do have I give you." Our life is more than the information we have learned. It is the substance, the very nature of Christ, that we have received from Him through our personal experience. Like Peter, we have something to give—the life and power of Christ—not just information to spread.

We can only give what we have. If we have suffered or walked with God through a hard time, then we have received confidence from the Holy Spirit Himself, and also comfort, assurance and boldness to give other people what they need:

> The Father of mercies and God of all comfort . . . comforts us in all our tribulation, that we may be able to comfort those who are in any trouble, with the comfort with which we ourselves are comforted by God.
>
> 2 Corinthians 1:3–4

This world desperately needs the Kingdom of God. God wants to use every believer as an instrument to exhibit the Kingdom. To lose our identity through passive behavior—dwelling on the past, feeling inferior or feeling inadequate and unworthy—only postpones the fact that God is waiting to use us to advance His Kingdom on the earth!

David Prevented Identity Theft

Maybe you feel like a well-kept secret. Actually, God has you in training until an appointed time. Maybe you feel as though you are not making a difference and your life is filled with menial tasks. Consider David. Earlier, we looked at the life of King David and how he pursued God's will for his life. But before David became Israel's king, he was God's well-kept secret. God's strategy was to "hide" David until the appointed time. Surely, David felt his life was ordinary.

He had the menial task of watching a few sheep while his brothers engaged in the excitement of battle.

However, during his time in the fields with the sheep, David became intimate with the Spirit of God. In the lonely hours, he cultivated and capitalized on the opportunity to commune with God. Reflecting back on that time, he wrote, "Trust in the LORD and do good; dwell in the land and cultivate faithfulness" (Psalm 37:3, NASB). David not only began to know God and experience His presence, but he obviously developed amazing confidence and boldness in his ongoing relationship with the Holy Spirit.

I love the fact that David had not reconciled himself to passivity. He was in hot pursuit of God, and his passion for God's Kingdom was top priority. He loved the presence of God and lived in a state of preparedness. Sure, he probably spent a lot of time practicing with his slingshot, hitting various targets as he spent those hours alone. Maybe he became so skillful that when the appointed time came, he saw Goliath's huge forehead as an easy target. Yet it is very evident that David intimately knew God. Look at his response when he appeared at the scene of the battle:

> David spoke to the men who stood by him, saying, 'What shall be done for the man who kills this Philistine and takes away the reproach from Israel? For who is this uncircumcised Philistine, that he should defy the armies of the living God?'

> 1 Samuel 17:26

David had no fear of Goliath, only an appalling anger that this giant mocked God's people. Even at a young age, David had embraced a spirit of boldness and confidence. There was no room in his life for passivity.

David's father sent him to check on his brothers at the battlefront, saying, "Take now for your brothers an ephah of this dried grain and these ten loaves, and run to your brothers at the camp. And carry these ten cheeses to the captain of their thousand, and see how your brothers fare, and bring back news of them" (verses 17–18).

When David arrived at the scene, the first thing he experienced was the atmosphere of fear and dread—the Israelites' response to Goliath taunting and mocking them. Such fear was contrary to David's heart—he was more familiar with the presence of God and His anointing. The presence of God far outweighed the fear.

Then David heard about the amazing reward to go to the man who would face the giant. The men of Israel said, "Have you seen this man who has come up? Surely he has come up to defy Israel; and it shall be that the man who kills him the king will enrich with great riches, will give him his daughter, and give his father's house exemption from taxes in Israel" (verse 25). What a powerful promise!

In the rest of this account, three attempts at stealing David's identity occurred, and each time, David's security as a son of God allowed him to prevent identity theft.

The first attempt to steal David's identity—a sibling. The first person who tried to steal David's identity was Eliab, his oldest brother. Eliab was obviously a control freak, insecure in his own identity and threatened by David:

> Eliab his oldest brother heard when he spoke to the men; and Eliab's anger was aroused against David, and he said, "Why did you come down here? And with whom have you left those few sheep in the wilderness? I know your pride and the insolence of your heart, for you have come down to see the battle."
>
> 1 Samuel 17:28

Like most control freaks, Eliab twisted the facts. He questioned David's motives and ridiculed his position as a shepherd. Then he accused him of pride. But Eliab was really describing himself. Those who control always project their own weaknesses on those they are trying to control. Eliab accused David of pride, but he was the one full of pride and an inflated ego. In today's terms, this is projection—putting the very thing we are guilty of onto someone else.

David shook off the identity theft attempt and said, "What have I done now? Is there not a cause?" (verse 29). Heaven must have rejoiced as David resisted the opportunity to become intimidated and offended.

The second attempt to steal David's identity—Saul. "When the words which David spoke were heard, they reported them to Saul; and he sent for him. Then David said to Saul, 'Let no man's heart fail because of him; your servant will go and fight with this Philistine'" (verses 31–32). When Saul heard these words, he tried to steal David's identity by defining him as too young: "You are not able to go against this Philistine to fight with him; for you are a youth, and he a man of war from his youth" (verse 33).

This is so typical of people who are controllers. Either they declare you too young or too old. I wonder when we are just the right age?

In defense, David referenced his résumé! He said to Saul,

> Your servant used to keep his father's sheep, and when a lion or a bear came and took a lamb out of the flock, I went out after it and struck it, and delivered the lamb from its mouth; and when it arose against me, I caught it by its beard, and struck and killed it. Your servant has killed both lion and bear; and this uncircumcised Philistine will be like one of them, seeing he has defied the armies of the living God. . . . The LORD, who delivered me from the paw of the lion and from the paw of the bear, He will deliver me from the hand of this Philistine.
>
> 1 Samuel 17:34–37

David knew his identity was in his anointing from God. And he knew the same power and anointing would deliver the Philistine into his hand.

Each of us has to deal with lions and bears. Lions represent those things that wage war against our soul, such as lust, greed, anger, pride and addictions. Bears represent the wounds we have experienced, plus emotions of discouragement and despair, that we all must overcome *before* we face the major giant in front of a crowd.

The third attempt to steal David's identity—Goliath. Even Goliath tried to strip David of his identity. He took one look at David and mocked him:

> When the Philistine looked about and saw David, he disdained him; for he was only a youth, ruddy and good-looking. So the Philistine said to David, "Am I a dog, that you come to me with sticks?" And the Philistine cursed David by his gods.
>
> 1 Samuel 17:42–43

Still, David knew who he was and understood his anointing. David's identity was in his fellowship with the Lord. No doubt he had spent countless hours intimately worshiping the Lord as he cared for the sheep. So when he spoke to Goliath, he spoke with authority: "You come to me with a sword, with a spear, and with a javelin. But I come to you in the name of the LORD of hosts, the God of the armies of Israel, whom you have defied" (verse 45).

With authority from the Lord, David declared that he would kill Goliath. He even described how. In effect, he was saying, "I'm going to kill you, but first I have a word from God for you!"

We need to be drenched with confidence in who God has called us to be as His children. This comes mostly from our fellowship with Him on a daily basis. Just as David grew in his relationship and fellowship with God while he sat alone in the field and watched the sheep, we can do the same during the time when we are still one of God's well-kept secrets. Soon enough it will become evident that our experience with the Lord will far outweigh any intimidation of the devil.

Jesus Knew His Identity

We can look to the Savior for another example of someone who understood His purpose and identity as a child of God. Jesus certainly was not passive, but He was not aggressive either. Instead, He was assertive in every situation.

When John baptized Jesus, immediately the heavens were opened and Jesus saw the Spirit of God descending on Him like a dove. Then a voice out of heaven declared, "This is My beloved Son, in whom I am well pleased" (Matthew 3:17). I believe Jesus needed to hear this affirmation from the Father Himself.

Immediately, Jesus was taken by the Holy Spirit into the wilderness to be tempted by the devil. And what was the first thing the devil tried to do? Challenge His identity! The devil said to Jesus, who had fasted forty days and was hungry, "If You are the Son of God, command that these stones become bread" (Matthew 4:3).

Of course, Jesus did not take the bait. Instead, He answered Satan by declaring the Word of God, "It is written, 'Man shall not live by bread alone, but by every word that proceeds from the mouth of God'" (Matthew 4:4).

Even the Son of God had His identity challenged! This is always the strategy of the enemy. He wants us to second-guess who we are.

As we endeavor to walk with God, worship and obey Him more, we will "hear" the Father affirming our identity. Just as the Father affirmed and reaffirmed Jesus' identity, we learn the art of soaking in God's presence by lying or sitting quietly before Him. Whatever way we seek God and wait upon Him, His very presence will affirm and confirm our identity.

Who Is Stealing Your Identity?

Just when we sense our true identity in the presence of God, that is the very moment when we must battle our tendency to surrender to passivity. Maybe someone in your life continually sabotages your identity. The challenge could come in the form of a lack of respect, or it could come as continual accusations or judgments from a spouse, a sibling, a relative or a co-worker. Or maybe someone continually reminds you of your past mistakes and failures. My answer to these accusations is that my failure is a place where I have been, but it does not define who I am. I have warts, but I am not a frog. Likewise, this is where you have to fight and refuse to accept someone else's definition of you. You have to declare instead who you are in Christ.

My father lived to be 95 years old, but even into the last months of his life, he still saw me as a ten-year-old child. In fact, sometimes I would travel around the world, then go visit my parents. As I sat at their kitchen table, Dad would speak to me in a tone that reduced me to a child.

While he did not mean to sound unloving, my father had a very dominating personality. Around my dad, I literally would forget momentarily who I was in Christ as I felt my authority and identity slipping away. I know Dad loved me in his own way, but he simply could not see me beyond the realm of being his little boy. This pattern happened every time I was around him, until I finally recognized that it was his problem and not mine. But I was the one who had to shake off the intimidation and reclaim my identity as a son of God.

The Past Does Not Define Us

Many of us have been trapped in a prison made of our past history—defined by a messy divorce, a financial failure or even a prison sentence. Although we may have experienced these or other failures, none of them define *who we are*. However, there will always be people who love to remind us of our past. We are the ones who must choose to be around people who celebrate us, not tolerate us.

That is the good news of the Gospel. God celebrates us as His children. He does not define us by what happened to us or by our mistakes or failures. He defines us by Himself. He calls us into a relationship with Him. He offers us an awesome and mind-boggling covenant—not a covenant that we even contribute to. He has called us into a covenant relationship with Him.

> For this is the covenant that I will make with the house of Israel after those days, says the LORD: I will put My laws in their mind and write them on their hearts; and I will be their God, and they shall be My people.
>
> Hebrews 8:10

The wonderful reality of this new covenant is that it has nothing to do with our performance. It is a covenant based on the relationship between God and Jesus—ratified by Jesus' sacrifice and His shed blood on the cross. It is good news!

Why does this covenant work? For one reason: "I will be merciful to their unrighteousness, and their sins and their lawless deeds I will remember no more" (verse 12). It is an ironclad covenant. It works even when we are having the worst day of our lives, because He extends mercy and answers prayer based on His performance, not ours.

How Do You Define Yourself?

Tattoos, piercings, bright blue painted hair and ill-fitting clothes are all part of a new generation's way of establishing its identity. This is not criticism, only recognition that every individual needs an identity and we are a society of people who do not know who we are. Teenagers even form gangs and commit vicious acts, willing to pay the price of murdering someone just to find acceptance and identity.

The pastor of a church where I was speaking recently told me of an incident at a board meeting. One of his board members, Bob, kept trying to discuss a subject not even remotely related to the business at hand. The pastor told him, "I'm sorry, but I feel this isn't the direction God wants us to take tonight. We're here to discuss these other matters."

Bob immediately stood up and left the room, declaring he was leaving the church. An hour later, the pastor told his wife what had happened. She reached Bob on his cell phone and lovingly said, "You're not leaving the church, are you?"

His response was, "Don't you know I'm worth millions of dollars?"

Bob's wealth was so entrenched in his identity that he expected everyone to bow to his agenda. Sadly, his wealth had become his identity. But what does being a millionaire have to do with prayer and seeking the mind of God?

I have heard that some successful churches have an unwritten rule that leaders will drive Lexus automobiles. Nothing is wrong with driving a Lexus. But do you know what I want to drive? The car that God leads me to drive! I currently drive an eleven-year-old convertible, and I love it.

We need to have the kind of relationship with God where we ask the Holy Spirit what to drive and where to live and what to do in all matters of life. Nothing is more exciting than being led by the Holy Spirit on these natural decisions. Why cave in to passivity and conform yourself to the opinions of others? Be yourself and let the Holy Spirit reveal to you your own uniqueness and individuality!

Maintaining Your Identity

If you have found your identity in your blessings and the ways God has prospered you, you have missed the point. Many who adhere to prosperity teachings have found their identities in the types of cars they drive or the houses and neighborhoods they live in. I certainly believe God loves to bless His people in many ways. But our identity should never be in the blessing. Our identity is found only in *the Blesser*.

The story of Job is familiar to most of us. Satan accused Job of only serving God because God had blessed him and made a hedge about him and his household. Satan said to God:

> Have You not made a hedge around him, around his household, and around all that he has on every side? You have blessed the work of his hands, and his possessions have increased in the land. But now, stretch out Your hand and touch all that he has, and he will surely curse you to Your face!
>
> Job 1:10–11

When God allowed the testing, Job was stripped of everything—his multitude of animals, his servants and even his sons and daughters. Ultimately, God even allowed Satan to strike Job's body. At this point, his wife said to him, "Do you still hold fast to your integrity? Curse God and die" (Job 2:9). But Job refused to sin or charge God with wrongdoing.

Many people facing Job's trials would have slipped into a passive role and assumed that God could not be trusted after all. Not Job! He responded to his wife, "You speak as one of the foolish women speaks. Shall we indeed accept good from God, and shall we not accept adversity?" (verse 10).

Job refused to give away his integrity or his identity. The blessing and health and provision of God were not Job's identity. *God was his identity.*

Identified As a Child of God

So many leaders place their identity in a certain title. Titles are not wrong, but neither are they who you are. Titles are simply the way you are identified before other people. Personally, I dislike titles. I have been in the ministry for more than three decades, and I prefer to be called Steve. That is

129

my name. No other description will add or subtract a single thing from my identity. I am Steve, a child of God.

Have you ever been to a hardware store to have a key duplicated? The worker takes your key over to a carousel full of hundreds of keys. He then chooses a key that most closely resembles the shape you want duplicated. The hundreds of keys on the carousel all have one common characteristic: They are blank. New and shiny, but blank. The employee takes the blank key and puts it in the machine next to your master key. The machine grinds the same notches into the blank key that are in the master key.

This is exactly how God changes our identity. We come to God as blank keys. As believers, we are new and shiny, but blank. The problem with blank keys is that they cannot open anything. Can you see the purpose of God in shaping us? As we line up with His life, He begins to make the same "notches" in us. The more we yield to Him, the more we become like Him. As the apostle Paul said:

> I have been crucified with Christ; it is no longer I who live, but Christ lives in me; and the life which I now live in the flesh I live by faith in the Son of God, who loved me and gave Himself for me.
>
> Galatians 2:20

The more our identity is in God as we are conformed to His image, the more our life becomes a key to open doors for other people. When Peter and John said "Look at us" to the crippled man, they were the keys God used to unlock his life into health and wholeness.

Whatever process or trial we have been through (or are going through), it is all well worth it because when we are shaped or notched by them, they cause our lives to more closely resemble God's plan for us. Then we are able to unlock and open doors for others.

Preventing Identity Theft

If you are a victim of Satan's attempts to steal your identity in Christ, what can you do about it? If the enemy is trying to stop you from becoming a key that God can use in the image of Jesus, what should you do? As we have explored in this chapter, you can do the following:

First, realize that your identity is in Christ rather than in your accomplishments, where you live or what you own. Make a decision to war against the temptation to adopt a passive attitude that says, "If it be Thy will." Why not passionately seek God for His perfect will and purpose for your life? Be assertive, as Jesus was! Dare to increase the Kingdom of God and do damage to the strategies and lies of the devil. As Ephesians 6 says, "Take up the whole armor of God, that you may be able to withstand in the evil day, and having done all, to stand. . . . Above all, [take] the shield of faith with which you will be able to quench all the fiery darts of the wicked one" (verses 13, 16).

How can you do that? Spend time in fellowship with God and meditate on His Word. As you study the Word, believe what God says about you and your life in Him as a justified, sanctified and blood-washed believer.

Second, remember that you are God's instrument. He has put a desire in you to be a blessing to everyone who crosses your path. Daily, you can ask Him to equip you with wisdom and the gifts of the Spirit so you can do as the apostle Peter directed:

> If anyone speaks, let him speak as the oracles of God. If anyone ministers, let him do it as with the ability which God supplies, that in all things God may be glorified through Jesus Christ.
>
> 1 Peter 4:11

You do not have to look far to find someone who needs prayer, encouragement or guidance from the Holy Spirit. God wants to use you as His instrument to deliver His message!

If your past is littered with the surrender of your identity and a life of aimlessness, do not despair. You can take your identity back! You can live assertively, respecting yourself and engaging in a fervent relationship with the Holy Spirit.

Understanding how Jesus exemplified and modeled an assertive life—and believing that He offers the same type of life to us—is the only way we can truly overcome our passive or aggressive behaviors. In the next section, we will explore more extensively how we can allow Christ to replace our passive spirit with a spirit of assertiveness.

Part 2

A God-Provided Solution

Living Assertively through Jesus Christ

What kind of life does God intend for us? Does He want us to be control freaks—aggressive and dominating Jezebels who will do anything to get our way? Or passive and avoidant Ahabs who will do anything to avoid confrontation? No. God wants us to allow the Holy Spirit to show us the shortcomings of these personalities so that we can recognize our need for change and enjoy the solution God has already provided through Jesus Christ.

10

Provoked from Passivity

On a warm July evening just a few weeks after my high school graduation, I received the shocking news that my closest friend, Tom, had drowned in a tragic accident. Still staggered over the news three days later, I served as one of the pallbearers at his funeral. The preacher talked about the love God had for all of us who were Tom's friends and were deep in grief. His words were so comforting—it was the anointing of the Holy Spirit, I know now. Although I grew up in church and was fortunate to be raised in a Christian family, I had never felt the Holy Spirit's presence. From that day on, I was filled with an insatiable hunger in my soul to find out more about this God who loved me. My life would never be the same.

I do not know whether or not anything happened to any of the other hundreds of young people in that sanctuary, but I was provoked! I knew my life was not right with God, and somehow my innermost being cried out to Him. Within weeks, God guided me into the paths of people who were sold out to Him and in tune with the Holy Spirit.

To this day, I am grateful to God for using the death of my friend to provoke me out of my slumber and passivity. As a result, He has led me on a journey that has taken me all over the world, and countless lives have been changed. Little will happen in our lives until we are provoked to change. In the stubbornness of our human nature, we willingly remain in a rut until we recognize that the Holy Spirit is waiting on us.

Proverbs 27:7 says, "A satisfied soul loathes the honeycomb, but to a hungry soul every bitter thing is sweet." I believe that bitter taste is change. Change always seems bitter, but when our passivity and spirit of slumber are provoked into action, countless lives are influenced. Change that seems bitter begins to taste sweet as we see how the Holy Spirit is leading us into glorious freedom from our past. It has often been said that the only thing permanent in life is change. Human nature has a tendency to resist change, but God is all about bringing change in our lives. He loves us too much to let us stay in bondage to anything.

Why Does God Provoke Us?

God wanted to bring a prophet into the world, but He had to prepare His instrument. According to the first chapter of 1 Samuel, there was a man named Elkanah who had two wives, Penninah and Hannah. Although Penninah had many children, Hannah had none because the Lord had closed her womb. Her rival, Penninah, began to chide Hannah and provoke her with severe agitation because she had no children. This provoking no doubt was extremely unpleasant, but it caused Hannah to begin to pray passionately for God to give her a child. It drove her to a point of desperation, and she cried out to God. Her desperation became so intense that Eli, the priest, thought she was drunk. But as a result of those desperate prayers, the great prophet Samuel was born, who would fulfill the purposes of God. Note that without the provocation, Hannah would never have prayed with such fervency and passion.

Think about it! If Penninah had not chided, agitated and severely provoked Hannah, then Hannah would not have been driven to the point of desperation and desire. She would not have cried out to God the way she did, and there would have been no prophet Samuel born for the purposes of God. Again, the ultimate manifestation of passivity is a refusal to change. We usually have no motivation to change without God's help. We need to be provoked because God intends to bring change in our lives "till we all come to the unity of the faith . . . to a perfect man, to the measure of the stature of the fullness of Christ" (Ephesians 4:13).

God loves us too much to let us stay where we are, and too many of us have allowed the Ahab spirit to have a chokehold on our destinies. God is all about change, and to change the way He wants us to, something in us must exhibit a willingness to confront every area the Holy Spirit puts His finger on. As I said at the start, this means we have to be brutally honest with ourselves. We have to boldly pray as David prayed, "Search me, O God, and know my heart; try me, and know my anxieties; and see if there is any wicked way in me, and lead me in the way everlasting" (Psalm 139:23–24).

Live a Provoking Lifestyle!

Years ago our family was traveling on a long trip. My fuel gauge was on empty, and I pulled off at an exit in a very dangerous part of a city. I quickly realized I had to get out of there, and I prayed fervently for enough fuel to get back on the interstate and drive to a safer place. I knew my tank was running on fumes, and I cannot describe my relief when I finally saw the welcome sign of a gas station. What a secure feeling it was to pump that gas and get back into the car with the tank showing full!

137

I believe many Christians (including me much of the time) live on "fumes." We are surviving rather than living with a full tank, ready to minister. But we ought not live in a survival mode where we are passive or aggressive or controlling. Rather, like Jesus, we are to be assertive, knowing our identity as a son or daughter of God—whom He justified and sanctified and declared worthy and righteous—and ready to influence a hurting world.

Now that a majority of people have their own cell phones, it is hard to believe that we ever lived without them. I have learned that a significant part of the cell phone is the charger. The phone will not work if it is not charged. Never have people from the phone company come to my door at night and declared that they were dropping by to charge my phone. They leave that responsibility up to me. If I do not charge my phone daily, it will look the same, still pretty and shiny—yet it will not work. It will be useless.

Equally, we have to take responsibility to charge our own spirits. Christian believers live irresponsibly when they do not charge and stir up the inner man. Paul stated, "That He would grant you, according to the riches of His glory, to be strengthened with might through His Spirit in the inner man" (Ephesians 3:16). He told Timothy to "stir up the gift of God which is in you through the laying on of my hands" (2 Timothy 1:6).

It is our responsibility to stir up our inner man and live life with a "charged battery," living toward God with an expectation that places a demand on His presence. If we do not charge up, when adversity comes into our lives we are unprepared, weakened and unstable. As a result, we cannot face the challenges in faith. That is why expectation is so important. It is the key to experiencing the miraculous. Passivity has to go, replaced with an awe and anticipation toward all God will do in and through us. But first, we have to discern, defeat and forsake the Ahab personality and break free from the spirit of passivity once and for all.

Tasting Provocation

A common practice in larger grocery stores is to station employees at various locations around the store to offer free samples to customers. Such samples are not meant to fill you up; they are meant to provoke you by letting you taste the product so you will be persuaded to buy it.

That is what the Holy Spirit does for us. He provokes us by letting us taste His presence. Tasting His presence is meant to provoke us to seek Him more and surrender more of ourselves to Him. God wants to give us far more than temporary satisfaction. We cannot get full on samples!

God is patient with us, but He does not honor the masks we wear or the dysfunction we exhibit. We might fool others, but we cannot fool Him. When we refuse to deal with our issues and continue to harden our hearts, He may take more drastic action:

> A certain man had a fig tree planted in his vineyard, and he came seeking fruit on it and found none. Then he said to the keeper of his vineyard, "Look, for three years I have come seeking fruit on this fig tree and find none. Cut it down; why does it use up the ground?" But he answered and said to him, "Sir, let it alone this year also, until I dig around it and fertilize it. And if it bears fruit, well. But if not, after that you can cut it down."
>
> Luke 13:6–9

The owner of the vineyard is God the Father, who is totally unsatisfied with the lack of fruit on the tree. His statement is, "Cut it down; why does it use up the ground?"

Are we using up space that God intended for fruitfulness? If we are not bearing fruit, the keeper of the vineyard, the Holy Spirit, longs to dig around and fertilize the soil we are in, to provoke us and give us a little more time to see if we respond. If we do not respond and are determined to stay in our old patterns of thought and behavior, the result will be a lack of fruit for the Kingdom. But, ever patient, God works to bring change in us, sometimes through provocation.

Which Emotion to Choose?

I like the Weight Watchers slogan, "Nothing tastes as good as thin feels." That is a powerful truth! We literally have to choose which emotion we want to live with—the emotion of enjoying the taste of unhealthy food, or the emotion of clothes fitting more loosely. This is how we must face life. Do we want to "enjoy" the emotion of telling someone off and have the temporary gratification of losing it when we feel like it? Or do we choose to respond to every situation God's way, surrendering to the Holy Spirit instead of to our flesh and refusing to react?

One of the most misunderstood principles in Scripture is that although the Holy Spirit is available to the believer, He waits to respond to our level of hunger and expectation. He does not respond just because we have a particular need. In fact, the Holy Spirit within us will remain dormant unless we learn to draw upon Him with expectation. A good example is when Jesus invited the disciples to get in the boat with Him and go to the other side of the lake. Rather than the voyage across going peacefully, a violent storm broke out:

> And suddenly a great tempest arose on the sea, so that the boat was covered with the waves. But He was asleep. Then His disciples came to Him and awoke Him, saying, "Lord, save us! We are perishing!"
>
> Matthew 8:24–25

So often we think that since the Lord knows our needs, He will automatically take care of our problems without being asked. Actually, He waits for us to "wake Him up." He slept through the disciples' dire circumstance. Yet once they found Him and stirred Him from sleep, He got up and dealt with their storm. Our God does not respond to storms and circumstances; He responds to us! It is our prayers that stir Him.

It is not enough to know that He dwells in us; we have to continually stir up our expectation of Him. Hosea told us, "Break up your fallow ground" (Hosea 10:12). We have to stir our hearts out of dullness and low expectations and break up that ground of unbelief, stirring ourselves with expectation and anticipation of what God will do.

Stirring One Another

The writer of Hebrews exhorts us to stir and provoke one another as well: "And let us consider one another in order to stir up love and good works" (Hebrews 10:24). We can stir the Spirit of God in one another by acts of kindness and love. Sometimes a phone call, sending someone a card or giving a word of encouragement will stir a person's life out of discouragement into faith toward God.

When my youngest daughter was around five years old, she learned to make brownies. She would get out the mixing bowl, put in the ready mix and add an egg, a little water and a little oil. Then she would say, "Daddy, please stir this for me." Recently it occurred to me how ridiculous it would be to declare that since all the ingredients are in the bowl, I could just put it in the oven. What an awful treat that would be if the unmixed ingredients were baked that way. It does not matter how right the ingredients are, they must be stirred!

In the Kingdom of God, we often have all the right ingredients in our lives. We have the gift of salvation, the baptism of the Holy Spirit, the gifts of the Holy Spirit, perhaps some testimonies of the power of God in our lives and even some prophetic words given to us. Yet even with all these precious ingredients, our responsibility is to stir up all of this with expectation, desire and faith. Hebrews gives an example where that did not happen: "For indeed the gospel was preached to us as well as to them; but the word which they heard did not profit them, not being mixed with faith in those who heard it" (Hebrews 4:2). And James said, "Thus also faith by itself, if it does not have works [corresponding action], is dead" (James 2:17).

Stirring Up the Holy Spirit

We can stir up the Holy Spirit by:

- **Prayer.** Intense, fervent prayer, both individually and corporately, will stir up the Holy Spirit. "And when they had prayed, the place where they were assembled together was shaken; and they were all filled with the Holy Spirit, and they spoke the word of God with boldness" (Acts 4:31).
- **Remembering.** When Jehoshaphat was under attack by three armies, he began to pray, calling to mind past victories: "Are You not our God, who drove out the inhabitants of this land before Your people Israel, and gave it to the descendants of Abraham Your friend forever?" (2 Chronicles 20:7).
- **Dialogue.** Getting together with a spouse, a friend or any believer to talk about the Lord and declare His goodness always stirs up the Holy Spirit within us. It is amazing how you begin to feel His presence, and you know He Himself is involved in the conversation.
- **Praise.** "But thou art holy, O thou that inhabitest the praises of Israel" (Psalm 22:3, KJV). Any time we praise Him, He is enthroned on our praises and His presence is stirred up. We can be discouraged or distracted, yet when we begin to praise Him, His presence arises and our perspective quickly changes.

142

God Is Waiting on Us!

If we are waiting on God to do something, we might want to examine whether God is waiting on us. He is waiting on us to stir up our inner man by inviting Him into our lives and stirring ourselves with expectation.

God is willing and desires to manifest Himself in awesome ways, but just as the disciples stirred Jesus from sleep, we must stir up our inner man. "But you, beloved, building yourselves up on your most holy faith, praying in the Holy Spirit" (Jude 20). We must take responsibility to stir up our inner man, stir up one another and stir up the Holy Spirit—declaring His ability and His willingness to give us what we need.

If these pages have provoked you to desire change, and if you are ready to see the Holy Spirit stirred up in your life, then it is time to move on. It is time to understand what assertiveness looks like and how you can leave passivity behind and live more assertively and victoriously.

11

Understanding Assertiveness

When I was growing up, my dad was the stereotypical workaholic, while my mom was hopelessly caught in a web of passivity. A very kind woman outwardly, my mom's behavior was predictably, "Do not confront under any circumstance." She passed this on to her children in both spoken and unspoken instruction and modeling. She often advised us, "Don't rock the boat." Or if someone insulted us, her answer was, "Don't say anything, just walk away." She epitomized someone who had long ago given in to passivity because of circumstances in her life. This was her way of avoiding external conflict and possibly conscious or subconscious internal stress—even at the cost of her identity.

I believe my mother's life-cycle pattern of passivity was visible by the time she reached the age of seven. It was exacerbated by the loss of her mother. At that young age, she quietly and passively resigned herself to facing conflict by internalizing it and not outwardly expressing her true feelings at any cost. Later in life, when she married my dad, I believe she totally surrendered to a life of passivity because of her earlier programming. His domineering and overbearing personality reinforced her passive behavior. Although he was not physically abusive, he was strongly opinionated and chauvinistic. My mom's passive pattern never changed. She simply gave up her God-given self-respect and self-trust. She repeatedly took the path of least resistance and solidified her passivity.

After struggling with my own passivity for many years, I realized that Mom passed on much of her passivity to me. I discovered that the pattern was strengthened again and again in nearly every relationship, especially those where conflict and disagreement were present. Being passive became a learned heart response as I followed what Mom had modeled. With passive traits like my mother's, I rarely felt free to express myself because I was always afraid of the potential conflict that might result. Because of the pattern set at an early age, I had learned to relinquish parts of my own personhood. This trapped me in a vicious downward spiral of self-condemnation—all because I did not understand how to stand my ground.

Tragically, this describes the inner life of many people—even many born-again people. It is a lifestyle of giving up our identity for the purpose of "peace at any price." However, this is not how God wants you and me to live. Instead, with assertive behavior, God wants us to stand up for ourselves, respect others and have them respect us in turn. That is a healthy assertiveness. Most people either have a passive nature (Ahab-like) or an aggressive nature (Jezebel-like), yet Jesus as our model and example was neither passive nor aggressive. Jesus was assertive. He dealt with people in an assertive manner, pointing out their choices but respecting their right to choose.

Assertiveness is more than something you do; it is who you are. It grows out of your maturity and your willingness to respect yourself. Assertive people choose not to play the victim and refuse to be helpless or hopeless, knowing they have choices and options. Assertive people speak clearly in a nonthreatening manner and exhibit self-respect while making their intentions clear. As Ruth N. Koch and Kenneth C. Haugk say in their book *Speaking the Truth in Love—How to Be an Assertive Christian*, "An assertive life style includes healthy thinking that challenges irrational beliefs, loves and believes the truth, and celebrates what God has done."[1]

As we learn to act assertively, we must learn to challenge our unhealthy thinking and irrational beliefs. Koch and Haugk say that some examples of beliefs in need of adjustment are:

- If someone is angry with me, it must be my fault.
- If others do not tell me I am a good person, then I must not be.
- It is my duty to make everyone happy and comfortable.
- It is my duty to please everyone all the time.
- Everyone ought to be nice to me.
- I should always be and act happy in spite of any hardship or trouble that comes my way.[2]

As we learn to live assertively, the way Jesus lived, we can overcome the Ahab spirit (and the Jezebel spirit) with His help. This involves taking a long, hard look at our responses or lack of responses and being brutally honest with ourselves.

Recognizing Ourselves

Everyone falls somewhere on a scale of passive to aggressive behavior. As you have been reading through this book, maybe

1. Ruth N. Koch and Kenneth C. Haugk, *Speaking the Truth in Love—How to Be an Assertive Christian* (St. Louis, Mo.: Stephen Ministries, 1992), 32.
2. Ibid., 33.

you have already taken a hard look at your own life and can recognize where you are on that scale:

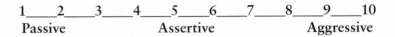

1___2___3___4___5___6___7___8___9___10
Passive   **Assertive**   **Aggressive**

We have explored in depth how passive and aggressive behaviors look. But let's sum up those traits in order to contrast them with assertiveness.

Passive behavior means nonresisting or nonacting—*passive* actually means "to suffer." Suffering is involved when confrontation is avoided. The problem with passive people is that they have a strong need for the approval of other people and a strong desire to avoid displeasure, disapproval or criticism.

Aggressive behavior moves against others (whereas passive behavior moves against self). Typically, aggressive types will stop at nothing to get their way, whether through insults, name-calling, blaming, domination, humiliating, put-downs, sarcasm, patronizing or even physical aggression.

Passive-aggressive personalities ultimately form from those who have been passive. Rage is often their prevailing attitude: "I don't get mad—I get even." In an extreme case, this can involve abuse such as physical violence and even murder. On a milder scale, emotions often explode over nothing.

Assertive behavior, on the other hand, seeks balance and maturity. In other words, we will not passively avoid confrontation, nor will we aggressively confront others in order to harm them. Instead, if someone offends us, we can tell them that it is not okay. We are doing ourselves and others a favor by letting them know where we stand. Hopefully this will heal our relationship.

Koch and Haugk write about being an assertive Christian: "Assertive individuals work for authentic personal relations, recognize the power of mutual respect, understand that their behavior influences the behavior choices of others, and know that they are contributing to the well-being of the whole community."[3]

Jesus Lived Assertively

Jesus demonstrated love and compassion. He always dealt in an assertive manner with people. He pinpointed their problems, yet at the same time showed them love and respect while presenting them with a good behavioral choice. "Jesus obeyed a higher law of love. That is why he healed on the Sabbath, respected and honored women, opposed the tyranny of misguided and evil church leaders, and honored those of low social status such as tax collectors and prostitutes," commented Koch and Haugk.[4]

Our best example to follow is Jesus, who always lived assertively. He lived the perfect life, neither succumbing to passivity nor yielding to aggressiveness. However, at times He chose to act aggressively, such as when he drove the money changers out of the Temple. But He was doing it for the sake of delivering His people from religious bondage. At times, He also chose to act passively, such as when He stood before Pontius Pilate. At that time, He was choosing to lay down His life for each of us and following the purpose of God to suffer and die in our place.

Jesus demonstrated assertiveness when He ministered to the woman caught in adultery (see John 8:1–12). Although her accusers wanted to use the Law as a reason to stone her, He treated her with respect. If they wanted her to stop sinning, their method was to kill her (which works every

3. Ibid., 40.
4. Ibid., 56.

time). Jesus also wanted her to stop, but offered her a new life instead. If He had been passive, He would have addressed her with love but not confronted her behavior, either saying nothing or perhaps suggesting, "Everyone has weaknesses, so just try harder to work on yours." If Jesus had been aggressive, He might have said something such as, "Hell is waiting for people like you."

However, Jesus dealt with the woman in an assertive manner. First, though, He dealt with her accusers. Although He could have easily used the situation to grandstand and expose all their sins and hypocrisy, instead He stooped down and began writing on the ground (probably listening to His Father). As He stood up, He spoke firmly and assertively: "He who is without sin among you, let him throw a stone at her first" (verse 7).

As her accusers walked away, Jesus spoke kindly to the woman: "Woman, where are those accusers of yours? Has no one condemned you?"

She answered, "No one, Lord."

And with compassion Jesus set her free, saying, "Neither do I condemn you; go and sin no more" (verses 10–11). What He was really saying was, "Repent, sinner!" But He said it with compassion and made a way for her to escape. That is assertiveness.

Jesus spoke similarly to the woman at the well—first by engaging her in conversation, then by lovingly pointing out her need: "Go, call your husband, and come here." When she replied that she had no husband, He spoke truth that was filled with hope: "You have well said, 'I have no husband,' for you have had five husbands, and the one whom you now have is not your husband; in that you spoke truly" (John 4:16–18).

The woman felt such hope and life coming from Him that she immediately went into town and declared to everyone, "Come, see a Man who told me all things that I ever did. Could this be the Christ?" (verse 29).

Loving Confrontation

Another person Jesus dealt with assertively was the wealthy young man who wanted to receive eternal life (see Mark 10:17–31). Jesus named six of the Ten Commandments, and the young man claimed he had kept all of them since his youth. Jesus recognized that the man's identity lay in his own riches and self-sufficiency, so He assertively put His finger on the problem. Looking at the man with love, Jesus said, "One thing you lack: Go your way, sell whatever you have and give to the poor, and you will have treasure in heaven; and come, take up the cross, and follow Me" (Mark 10:21).

The young man walked away sorrowfully because he had a great many possessions. It is noteworthy, however, that Jesus did not try to control the young man's actions or decisions. He showed him respect, knowing the man had to make his own life choices and live with the consequences.

Of course, it is easy to see how Jesus acted assertively, but can we really live that way? Peter and Joanna went out to a movie one night, giving instructions to their thirteen-year-old daughter, Carla, to do the dishes before watching television. When they arrived home around midnight, they found the dirty dishes untouched in the sink. Peter went into Carla's bedroom and touched her shoulder, telling her to get up. "You didn't finish the dishes like you were asked, so you're going to do them now." Carla tried to roll over and go to sleep, but her dad lovingly said, "No, you are going to get up and finish them like you promised." No harsh words were spoken, but Peter and Joanna sat at the kitchen table and watched while Carla finished the chore. Instead of scolding her in the morning or doing the dishes themselves, they acted assertively, insisting that Carla fulfill her responsibility.

Joshua and Heather's teenage son, Nathan, was happy to have his first car. Although it was several years old, it was in fairly good condition. Nathan, at sixteen, was very proud of it. Joshua reminded Nathan a number of times that because it

151

was an older car, he needed to check the oil regularly. Nathan did not take his dad seriously, and the engine ran low on oil and burned up. Joshua was sympathetic, but told Nathan he would have to be without a car until he saved up enough money to have the engine repaired. Nathan was not at all happy, but his parents were firm, allowing him to learn that bad choices and irresponsibility have consequences.

Living with Innocence

Living assertively means we must always choose to eat from the Tree of Life, and not from the Tree of Knowledge of Good and Evil. Christians who live passively or aggressively are eating from the wrong tree. In the Garden of Eden, God gave Adam and Eve instructions that they could eat from any tree in the Garden with the exception of the Tree of Knowledge of Good and Evil. When the serpent deceived Eve and she ate of the fruit of the forbidden tree, and Adam did as well, their eyes were opened. Not only did they realize they were naked, but they became judges. Adam was the first judge in the Bible, saying to God, "The woman whom You gave to be with me, she gave me of the tree, and I ate" (Genesis 3:12). He was saying, in effect, "I judge that this is Your fault and her fault."

Many agree that sin and disobedience separated Adam and Eve from their relationship with God. But equally significant, they lost their innocence. From this point on, they were judging everything from their own limited perspective, not from God's. Before the Fall, there was no need to judge anything because there was no knowledge of good and evil, just a simple trust in God.

When we live without innocence, we put ourselves in charge of judging every situation instead of letting God be the judge. We are eating from the wrong tree, the Tree of Knowledge of Good and Evil! Therefore, when we interact with other people, we act passively or aggressively. When we judge another person, we either "lose it" and become aggressive, or we turn it on ourselves (blame ourselves) and passively ignore whatever just happened.

However, once we are Christians and know we have been reconciled to God through the sacrifice of His Son, we must realize that we need to be restored to the innocence Adam and Eve originally experienced in the Garden. If we live with innocence, letting God be the judge, we can assertively deal with and confront each situation. Jesus put a high premium on innocence. He said, "Be shrewd as serpents and innocent as doves" (Matthew 10:16, NASB); "Unless you are converted and become as little [innocent] children, you will by no means enter the kingdom of heaven" (Matthew 18:3); and "I thank You, Father, Lord of heaven and earth, that You have hidden these things from the wise and prudent and revealed them to [innocent] babes. Even so, Father, for so it seemed good in Your sight" (Luke 10:21).

When we live assertively, we are choosing life. When Paul and Silas were thrown into the inner prison and put in stocks after being beaten until they had many stripes, they had to make a decision (see Acts 16:16–40). If they were eating from the Tree of Knowledge of Good and Evil, they would have judged what had happened to them, concluding it was evil and aggressively asking God to bring quick judgment on those who beat them. Or they could have acted passively, saying, "It must have been God's will; we're just sinners saved by grace." Or sarcastically, "Is *this* what we get for serving God?" Instead, Paul and Silas chose life! At midnight, they began to sing. All the prisoners were listening to them, and God caused an earthquake and everyone's chains were loosed. They were free to go! Again, Paul and Silas chose life. Rather than having the attitude, "They got what they deserved," Paul yelled out in the darkness to the jailer, "Do yourself no harm, for we are all here" (verse 28). The end result was that the jailer and his entire family were saved and came to know the Lord Jesus Christ.

What does it mean to choose life? How do you and I get free? First, we have to make a conscious and daily decision to choose life in every situation. For example, say you are driving and someone in another car makes an ugly gesture. If you are eating from the Tree of Knowledge of Good and Evil, you will judge the person as rude and will react with anger (aggressively) toward the person. Or you might blame yourself and take the attack personally (passively), letting it ruin your day. However, if you are eating from the right tree, the Tree of Life, you will recognize that the person's rudeness has nothing to do with you—it is his or her problem. You might even think, *I don't think I did anything wrong, but if I did, I'm sorry.*

When you choose life, you are choosing to remain innocent and let God be the judge. You can observe every situation, but you acknowledge that judging another person and his or her motives is something only God is qualified to do.

How to Confront Assertively

Assertiveness has so much to do with "speaking the truth in love" (Ephesians 4:15) and also with having a healthy respect for yourself. It is okay to confront a person who has hurt you, but it does not have to occur in a hateful or aggressive manner.

Jesus told us if our brother sins against us, we can rebuke him (see Luke 17:3). This does not mean to take his head off. The word *rebuke* comes from the word *epitamao*, which comes from two Greek words meaning "upon" and "to fix a value or to honor." Or one might define it "to charge strongly." In his book *How to Stop the Pain*, Dr. James Richards of Impact Ministries maintains that pain is inevitable, but suffering is optional. He addresses the issues of emotional wounds and pain, and looks at the forces that turn us into victims. He tells us not only how to forgive, but how to live free from judging others:

> It could be that rebuking is nothing more than making a person aware of the *value* of their actions. To say to a person, "I know *why* you did this" is not a rebuke, but a judgment. All we can say in a rebuke is this: "This is what you did, and this is the effect it had on me." Nothing more, nothing less. We cannot attach significance. We cannot use that action to judge what kind of a person he or she is. We can tell the person that he or she has done this thing often. But we cannot judge the intent. Passive people usually let an offense slide, and "stuff" the pain and emotions. But we simply can say, "This is what you have done; this is how it affected me."[5]

Breaking the Power of Pain

Our motive for any rebuke is to bring the other person to a recognition of wrongdoing and hopefully to repentance. Jesus said of forgiving another, "And if he sins against you seven times in a day, and seven times in a day returns to you, saying, 'I repent,' you shall forgive him" (Luke 17:4).

Dr. Richards also points out in his book,

> Our goal should be to bring the person to repentance. The goal cannot be punishment. Punishment is the penalty that we think a person deserves based on our judgment. Judgment precedes vengeance. Until we pass judgment, we have no desire for vengeance. Remember, we have no right to vengeance. God says vengeance belongs to Him alone (Romans 12:19).[6]

In other words, if you are in a situation where your spouse says something that humiliates or embarrasses you, you need

5. Dr. James B. Richards, *How to Stop the Pain* (New Kensington, Penn.: Whitaker House, 2001), 26.
6. Ibid.

to be assertive and rebuke him or her. You can do this in the spirit of reconciliation and not hate, which would only drive a larger wedge between you. You can "rebuke" by saying that you need to talk. Then say something such as, "Yesterday, we were with the Smiths and you interrupted me several times right in the middle of my sentences. Since then, I have felt very hurt, and I need you to know how this crushed my feelings."

Such a statement is not an accusation, but is assertively telling your partner that because of his or her action, you are feeling pain. This gives your spouse an opportunity to see the hurt he or she caused and (hopefully) apologize for the poor behavior. The end result is that you feel healed, and you have released your spouse from the anger you felt toward him or her.

Now that we understand what assertiveness is, we can next look at how to act assertively and how to pursue assertiveness—even when our natural tendencies tempt us toward acting passively or aggressively.

12

Pursuing Assertiveness

I have a friend, Andy, who became the proverbial people pleaser just to keep his marriage intact. His passive nature and longing for acceptance so blinded him that he could not see how he had become easy prey for his manipulative wife. He spent all his time trying to please her, while at the same time giving her tacit permission to use anything to get what she wanted. Andy's wife never showed him true respect, but she did "throw him a crumb" once in a while. In essence, whenever she needed something from him, she acted extraordinarily sweet. Of course, Andy was so overjoyed with her sweetness (lying to himself on some level, since he had to know it was only temporary) that he would do anything she asked. As soon as his wife got what she wanted, her coldness toward him quickly returned and she disrespected him all the more, using him to get what she wanted.

These patterns of behavior between them took place again and again, keeping Andy in bondage for years, until one day a wise counselor got through to him. The counselor asked Andy, "How long is it going to take you to realize that no matter how much you do for her, she isn't going to love you until you love and respect yourself and use your God-given anger on a daily basis to establish and set boundaries?"

With their marriage on the verge of collapse, Andy finally stood up to his wife and stopped being a doormat. When he took a stand, it was not exactly pleasant, but his life began to change drastically. Indeed, God was waiting for him to act more assertively. Heaven must stand up and cheer when the passive person finally says, "Enough! You're not going to do this to me anymore."

If you see yourself in Andy, you might be struggling with a fear of other people or a lack of respect for yourself. You might even be rebelling—perhaps subconsciously—against the authority God has given you. However, God wants you and me to possess the vision He has already given us, to "go in and possess the land of which the LORD swore to your fathers" (Deuteronomy 8:1). In other words, God wants to do far more than simply redeem us. He wants to restore all that the enemy has stolen from us. But this requires our cooperation. God desires that we live our lives before Him with such a sense of purpose and destiny that we will influence others and increase His Kingdom. We can only live this way when we learn to live assertively.

Passive people rarely have a vision to conquer anything, much less to take a stand when opposed—their only goal is survival. However, God wants His children to become assertive people who are as "wise as serpents" yet as "harmless [innocent] as doves" (Matthew 10:16).

Learning Assertiveness

Pursuing assertiveness requires relearning a lot of behaviors. Old patterns of passivity are not easily overcome. Sometimes passivity is learned or inherited behavior, but whatever its origins, it definitely must be dealt with if the person desires to have a normal life.

A good example of assertiveness is caller ID. I used to think that I had to answer every phone call. Now I recognize that caller ID is one of the greatest things ever invented! Previously, I willingly answered every call, interrupting my schedule to appease every caller. But now, when I see who is calling, I can choose to not answer, knowing I can return the call at my convenience. This is a way of respecting myself and freeing myself from the lie that I need to please everyone.

Assertiveness has a lot to do with respecting yourself by taking a stand. For example, maybe you are married to someone who is chronically late. This may be a real thorn in your side, but you continue to put up with the behavior even though being late causes you discomfort and embarrassment. Assertiveness requires that you make a positive decision such as saying, "I am leaving here tomorrow at nine o'clock. If you are not ready, I will meet you there."

Another example of assertiveness would be to say to a messy roommate, "I'm frustrated when you leave dirty dishes in the sink because not only do they draw bugs, but I have to clean them up the following day. I would appreciate it if you would take the time to rinse them off." An aggressive, accusatory statement would be, "I can't believe how lazy you are not to take the time to rinse off your dishes." That is counterproductive and will cause the person to resent and resist you. A passive attitude would be to say nothing and always clean up the dishes yourself, but anger would build as you push feelings of resentment inside. The most foolish thing you can do is not communicate. It is never wise to repress your feelings—the fallout of your emotions and mental health is too big a price to pay.

From these examples, we can see why a healthy assertiveness protects our spiritual and emotional health.

Honesty

To live assertively, it is vitally important that you be honest about your feelings. Passive people tend to disguise what they feel because they fear a lack of acceptance. Often they resort to hints or make vague or less-than-truthful statements that lead to confusion.

For example, perhaps plans are being made to get together on Thursday, but you really prefer Friday because Thursday is a busy day for you. However, you cannot quite speak up and say that Friday would be much better for you, so you reluctantly agree to meet on Thursday. Or perhaps you are meeting someone for lunch. They suggest Mexican food, but you do not like Mexican food. However, rather than plainly saying, "I don't like Mexican food" or suggesting another restaurant, you come up with objections such as, "It's too far from here" or "Maybe they are closed."

This is not just pop psychology about passivity. Jesus Himself said, "Let your 'Yes' be 'Yes,' and your 'No,' 'No.' For whatever is more than these is from the evil one" (Matthew 5:37). Many times, passive behavior can harm a relationship if a person keeps switching from yes to no and back again. As Koch and Haugk say in *Speaking the Truth in Love*:

> Responding to requests is based primarily on two rights: the right others have to make a request, and the right you have to grant, refuse, or negotiate another's request. Along with these two rights goes your right to all the necessary information you need to be fully aware of the nature of the request.[1]

Say *I*, Not *You*

It is typical to accuse people when we are frustrated, so it is wise to avoid that temptation by always using *I* statements

1. Koch and Haugk, 121.

when addressing an issue. This puts us in a place of responsibility for the statements we make, so we cannot be blamed for recklessly accusing someone of something. Using *I* declares that I alone am responsible for the statement I am making. A good example of this would be, "*I* get frustrated when you spend all the time talking on your cell phone when we have an evening together." This is so much better than saying, "*You* are so selfish and insensitive." Another example is, "*I* am upset that you won't help me do the dishes, and *I* would like you to pitch in and help tonight." This is far better than saying, "If *you* loved me at all, *you* would help." That, of course, is a manipulative statement meant to motivate the other person with guilt and shame. Use statements such as, "*I* was so hurt when you didn't call like you promised," instead of "*You* were so inconsiderate not to call when I was waiting all evening." *I* statements help reinforce what we want without making accusations.

Notice that in addition to *I*, you can always start by stating how you feel (frustrated, upset, hurt), because no one can say that your feelings are not valid. At the same time, it is also important to tell the other person what you want. For example, "I want you to stop making fun of my nose," or "I would rather eat out tonight instead of tomorrow night," or "I want you to look at me when we are discussing this subject." Again, you are not trying to hurt people or make them feel bad; you are trying to get them to realize the hurt you feel and to take responsibility for changing their behavior.

Avoid Accusations

It is tempting to use accusatory words when someone disappoints us. But being assertive means we can point out poor behavior without accusing the person. For example, if your teenager locks the keys in the car, instead of saying, "I can't believe how careless and stupid you were; now we'll have to

161

call a tow truck," it would be better to say, "I'm so disappointed that you locked the keys in the car. Next time, make sure you're holding the keys before you shut the door."

Or maybe you have a friend who accuses you of being stupid. A passive person might say, "Maybe I am stupid," or just walk away feeling wounded. But rather than receive that demeaning comment, it would be better to say, "I feel deeply hurt when you call me stupid. I expect you to apologize to me and stop calling me stupid in the future." If you do not stand up to this kind of behavior, I guarantee you that such demeaning statements will continue.

How do you respond when someone accuses you of something? You probably immediately want to defend yourself. Never use sarcasm. Sarcasm is always aggressive. The Greek root of the word *sarcasm* means "flesh-tearing." Sarcasm is never profitable. If someone has kept you waiting, a sarcastic statement might be, "Are you sure you are not too busy to help me?" said in a cutting way. Instead, it would be better to say, "I'm disappointed you took so long to get here, so can we hurry up and get this project done?"

Don't Apologize; Stand Your Ground

Apologizing for making a legitimate request is typical of passive people. They will say, "I am sorry and I don't mean to be difficult, but you didn't finish repairing my car by Friday afternoon like you promised."

Why would you apologize in such a situation? An "I'm sorry" on your part is a statement that excuses the other person for behaving irresponsibly. It would be better to say, "Mr. Brown, I recall that you promised to complete the work today, but you did not, so I definitely want it finished by tomorrow morning." You can make known your legitimate request in an assertive manner without using a weak statement to take ownership for someone else's issues.

You must be clear about what you want. Passive people have a difficult time saying no. Often when they speak to a salesman, for instance, they will let a fast talker change their minds for them. In the process of making a purchase, a salesman might try to talk you into buying extra features. At this point, it is good to be firm and say, "No, *this* is what I need." Or perhaps if you return a defective item, the salesman might try to talk you into replacing it. This is when you assertively say, "No, I would just like a refund."

If someone is acting grumpy, the classic reaction of an aggressive person would be to say, "Well, excuuuse me!" The classic reaction of a passive person would be to say nothing and shove the rejection deep within, letting the grumpy behavior pass. But a good assertive statement would be, "I sense that you're upset with me—is there something you'd like to talk about?"

God always encourages us to respond assertively in situations, whereas the devil wants us to react passively or aggressively. We passive people get ourselves in trouble and line up for more hurt when we react to things rather than responding to them assertively. We react by apologizing when others are at fault, letting others talk us into or out of things, and allowing poor behavior to go unchallenged. We need to stand our ground without apology instead.

Challenging Jezebel or Ahab

We often mistakenly think we can change a Jezebel or an Ahab. The only thing we can really do when dealing with either is to challenge them, assertively letting them know that their behavior is unacceptable and that we will not let them do that to us anymore. The same holds true of challenging ourselves. If God is helping me recognize that I am a controlling Jezebel or a passive Ahab, I need to seek deliverance from that behavior, asking Him to reveal the root of it and set me free.

Most of us who have dealt with a person with a Jezebel spirit agree that he or she needs deliverance. A person with the Ahab spirit needs deliverance as well. The problem is that we cannot deliver someone against his or her will. This is a hugely significant point. While there is little question that demonic influence is present, most Jezebels are so wounded and insecure that it is rare for them to admit that they are wrong, let alone that they need deliverance. Ahabs seem far more willing to admit they are wrong, because they feel a need for connection and intimacy—but they are often stubbornly resistant about leaving their comfort zone since they want everyone to like them.

Praying for people to be delivered of demons when they are not demonstrating heartfelt repentance and a genuine desire to be free is not wise. They have not closed the door to their sin, which leaves an opportunity for the demons to take possession again. Jesus said:

> When an unclean spirit goes out of a man, he goes through dry places, seeking rest; and finding none, he says, "I will return to my house from which I came." And when he comes, he finds it swept and put in order. Then he goes and takes with him seven other spirits more wicked than himself, and they enter and dwell there; and the last state of that man is worse than the first.
>
> Luke 11:24–26

Often a controlling nature occurs on both an emotional level and a spiritual level. On an emotional level the person needs healing, which will be determined by his or her willingness to receive it. Many times the person is so wounded that he or she is extremely defensive, claiming to be the victim and quickly blaming everyone else for the issues at hand. On a spiritual level the person needs to repent of self-centeredness and show a willingness and humility to have a teachable spirit. If demonic activity is present, then it is a spiritual problem and the person must acknowledge his or her sinful behavior and truly repent before deliverance can come.

In my experience, people whose behavior is demonic in origin have opened the door to a demon at some point. This may be traced back to childhood. Perhaps because of severe rejection or abuse, the person made a vow against a perpetrator and thus opened the door to demonic influence. Matthew 7:1 warns us, "Judge not, that you be not judged." Some believe that we can inherit a curse from our parents, and we can activate that curse by making a vow and a judgment against our parents. Such a vow or judgment might be, "I will never keep a messy house like my mother," or "I will never have a temper like my father." When we make such vows, we open a door through which demonic spirits can find a place to attach.

I have seen instances where those with a strong Jezebel spirit agree to counseling, but soon it becomes obvious that they are only there to convince a counselor they are right. If the counselor is not discerning, he or she might enable the Jezebel spirit by agreeing or sympathizing with the controller. Those with a Jezebel spirit can be extremely convincing, and frankly, they can lie very persuasively.

A couple in need of marriage counseling approached a pastor friend of mine. The husband, Jason, was a strong Jezebel controller. His wife, Karen, was a passive Ahab. Jason was very demanding of Karen's time and always wanted her available to him, but he would leave and spend time with his friends, never considering her needs. However, Karen was lazy and would leave the house a mess, unconcerned about daily chores even though she did not have a job outside the home.

After listening to them both vent their frustrations, my pastor friend spoke very wisely, saying, "Both of you have your point of view. I can't help you unless you both admit you are wrong. The only way counseling works is if you both know you are wrong and God is right." Then he pointed out to them that God's Word is the standard, and their willingness to follow the Word of God as their authority was the key to working out their problems.

Using Others to Stop Our Pain

Those of us with passive personalities wrongly expect others to stop our pain. Melody Beattie, the well-known author of several books on codependency, wrote the following in *The Language of Letting Go: Daily Meditations for Codependents*:

> Our happiness is not a present someone else holds in his or her hands. Our well-being is not held by another to be given or withheld at whim. If we reach out and try to force someone to give us what we believe he or she holds, we will be disappointed. . . . The person didn't hold it. He or she never shall. That beautifully wrapped box with the ribbon on it that we believed contained our happiness that someone was holding—it's an illusion!
>
> In those moments when we are trying to reach out and force someone to stop our pain and create our joy, if we can find the courage to stop flailing about and instead stand still and deal with our issues, we will find our happiness.
>
> Yes, it is true that if someone steps on our foot, he or she is hurting us and therefore holds the power to stop our pain by removing his or her foot. But the pain is still ours. And so is the responsibility to tell someone to stop stepping on our feet.
>
> Healing will come when we're aware of how we attempt to use others to stop our pain and create our happiness. . . .
>
> We will see that, all along, our happiness and our well-being have been in our hands. We have held that box. The contents are ours for the opening.
>
> *God, help me remember that I hold the key to my own happiness. Give me the courage to stand still and deal with my own feelings. Give me the insights I need to improve my*

relationships. Help me stop doing the codependent dance and start doing the dance of recovery.[2]

Poor Substitute

If you are a passive person, perhaps you never learned to assert yourself. You may be known as a gentle, peaceful person, but passivity is often mistaken for a gentle and peaceful spirit. However, nothing could be further from the truth! Passivity is a poor substitute for gentleness and peace. Outwardly, passivity looks like a peaceful personality. But inwardly, passivity is a personality that has learned to avoid confrontation at the cost of its own personhood. Passivity looks a lot like peace or gentleness, but it is actually compliant and subservient. A passive personality is like an artificial piece of fruit—it may look good on the outside, but it cannot compare to the real thing.

The Old Testament account of Eli provides a vivid example of someone who possessed the artificial fruit of passivity. He served in the Temple of God with a less-than-fervent passion for following God's commands. And he failed to confront his sons for their sins against the Lord and against the people.

God was not pleased with Eli, so He sent a message of judgment through the young prophet Samuel to address the issue:

> In that day I will perform against Eli all that I have spoken concerning his house, from beginning to end. For I have told him that I will judge his house forever for the iniquity which he knows, because his sons made themselves vile, and he did not restrain them.

> 1 Samuel 3:12–13

2. Melody Beattie, *The Language of Letting Go: Daily Meditations for Codependents* (San Francisco: Harper & Row, 1990), 99.

When Eli heard this, his response was remarkable. It reeked of passive indifference. Eli said, "It is the LORD. Let Him do what seems good to Him" (verse 18).

It almost defies belief that Eli would respond so nonchalantly after hearing God's impending judgment on his household. We also can infer that Eli followed this same pattern when he failed to confront his sons.

A normal response might have been to call on God to reverse His decision, or at least to appeal to God for mercy! Instead, Eli's answer showed classic passivity: "I won't challenge, and I won't respond fully." Eli opted for the least confrontational path and the one less likely to produce rejection. The result of that avoidance option was destruction.

What Lies Ahead

Have you seen yourself in the stories throughout this part of the book? Maybe someone has assaulted your self-worth. Maybe you have experienced a difficult childhood that has kept you in a prison of passivity. Or maybe you can see a part of yourself in those who allowed others to take advantage of their people-pleasing nature. Maybe you can see yourself in my mother, who believed she must keep the peace at any price and never rock the boat under any circumstances. Do you see yourself reeling from the effects of a passive spirit?

You do not have to live as a victim of passivity any longer! God does not want us to live the way Ahab did because passive behaviors rob us of God's purpose and destiny for us. The days of giving our power away are over. With the Holy Spirit's help, we can break the bondage of a passive spirit. When we follow the example of Jesus and live assertively, we will discover that it is time to enjoy life and live in victory! That is what part 3 of this book will show us—the benefits of living assertively.

A Life of Freedom

Enjoying the Benefits of Assertive Living

We can break free from the bondage of passivity through the work and example of Jesus Christ. Empowered and emboldened by the ministry of the Holy Spirit, we can confidently live out our lives with the assertive nature God desires for us. Assertive living promotes both our own growth and the increase of His Kingdom.

13

God Loves a Thankful Heart

Robert was married to Jennifer, who was a strong avoidant personality and never expressed gratitude for anything. During the entire duration of their marriage, no matter how much he did for her, she would merely grunt a barely audible "thanks" (if that) and then within a short time demand that he do more. This occurred over many years and finally climaxed at the point when he agreed to help her parents buy a home. This time he fully expected a huge display of gratitude from Jennifer, especially because he could have spent the money on other things. But she never acknowledged his sacrifice. This hurt Robert deeply, but consistent with his passive nature, he hid his feelings and did not say anything.

However, a few months later, her parents needed more financial help, which Jennifer again asked Robert to provide. He answered her by saying, "I'm happy to help them, but I never got a thank-you for the home I bought for your parents."

Jennifer replied, "They loved the home."

"I don't mean your parents," Robert said. "I mean that I never received a thank-you from you!"

At that, Jennifer exploded and fumed relentlessly about how terrible it was for him to request a thank-you from her. She refused to back down from her blatantly ungrateful attitude and did not offer him a "thank-you" for buying her parents a house. This was the last straw for Robert, who finally stopped his passive behavior of constantly trying to please her. He realized that he was dealing with a Jezebel personality, and he began to take a stand. Robert not only saw his own weakness, but he also saw the relentless demands of her Jezebel spirit.

He realized that he had never received a heartfelt thank-you from his wife in all the years of their marriage. The only time she would temporarily drop her coldness and be sweet was when she wanted him to buy her something. As Robert addressed his passivity and began to act assertively, Jennifer became angrier and angrier, furious that he would not bow at her feet or give her more things. Robert had finally turned his back on his passivity. He began to respect himself and refused to play the servant any longer.

Jezebels are takers. They are not thankful people, and they rarely acknowledge the input and help of anyone. They feel that everyone owes them, and they have no problem being the recipient of everyone else's generosity. The book of Romans makes a significant reference to those who are unthankful:

> Although they knew God, they did not glorify Him as God, nor were thankful, but became futile in their thoughts, and their foolish hearts were darkened. Professing to be wise, they became fools.
>
> Romans 1:21–22

Aggressive individuals see no need to be thankful because out of their woundedness they have an attitude of entitlement. Passive personalities, on the other hand, can become so need-oriented that they, too, refuse to live with an attitude of gratefulness. But when we learn to live assertively, we free ourselves to be grateful for God's provision and blessing in our lives.

Thankfulness Is Key

Thankfulness is one of the most overlooked areas in the life of many believers today. Often, we fail to remember and appreciate what God has done. In the Old Testament, memorials were set up to keep later generations from forgetting how the hand of God moved.

Most of us are familiar with the story of Gideon and how God worked such a mighty miracle through him to restore the country that had been controlled by the Midianites. Actually, God had turned the Israelites over to the Midianites because of their evil deeds, but He delivered them when they cried out to Him. "Then the children of Israel did evil in the sight of the LORD. So the LORD delivered them into the hand of Midian for seven years" (Judges 6:1). But He heard their cry and raised up Gideon to deliver them. Yet at the end of Gideon's life, there was no recognition given to him or his family, and people went back to their old ways of worshiping idols:

> Now Gideon the son of Joash died at a good old age, and was buried in the tomb of Joash his father, in Ophrah of the Abiezrites.
>
> So it was, as soon as Gideon was dead, that the children of Israel again played the harlot with the Baals, and made Baal-Berith their god. Thus the children of Israel did not remember the LORD their God, who had delivered them from the hand of all their enemies on every side; nor did they show kindness to the house of Jerubbaal (Gideon) in accordance with the good he had done for Israel.
>
> Judges 8:32–35

God had gone to so much trouble to deliver the Israelites from the Midianites and brought such an incredible victory, but as soon as their deliverer (Gideon) was dead, they quickly turned back to other gods.

Nothing much seems to change in human nature. We turn to God in times of crisis but quickly resort to our former ways as soon as the pressure is off. For us, the old ways might be neglecting our prayer life, losing our passion or surrendering to old habits. How many times do we take God and His power of deliverance for granted? Just as it was in ancient Israel, it is so easy for us today to let the intervention of God go unnoticed and unacknowledged. Have you ever stopped to take an inventory of all the blessings God has allowed to come your way?

Do Not Forget God's Blessings!

In the book of Deuteronomy, as God blessed His people with great increase, the Spirit of God gave them a blatant reminder about being thankful:

> So shall it be, when the LORD your God brings you into the land of which He swore to your fathers, to Abraham, Isaac, and Jacob, to give you large and beautiful cities which you did not build, houses full of all good things, which you did not fill, hewn-out wells which you did not dig, vineyards and olive trees which you did not plant—when you have eaten and are full—then beware, lest you forget the LORD who brought you out of the land of Egypt, from the house of bondage.
>
> Deuteronomy 6:10–12

What a warning from God not to forget that He is the source of all the blessings. I think one of the greatest flaws we have as Christians is how quickly we depend on God when we are in trouble, yet how quickly we "unplug" from His presence when the blessings are flowing.

When I was a pastor, I met so many people who would seek God intensely during difficulties and ask His help with things like the pain of financial shortages, marriage troubles or job issues. Yet when the storm ceased, they would revert back to a state of comfort and indifference concerning His promises. We need to stay thankful and diligent through blessed times as well as through storms.

And we desire that each one of you show the same diligence to the full assurance of hope until the end, that you do not become sluggish, but imitate those who through faith and patience inherit the promises.

Hebrews 6:11–12

A Poor Memory

Israel had the same problem of easily forgetting the goodness of God:

> Our fathers in Egypt did not understand Your
> wonders;
> They did not remember the multitude of Your
> mercies.
> But rebelled by the sea—the Red Sea.
>
> Nevertheless He saved them for His name's sake,
> That He might make His mighty power known.
> He rebuked the Red Sea also, and it dried up.
> So He led them through the depths,
> As through the wilderness.
> He saved them from the hand of him who hated
> them,
> And redeemed them from the hand of the enemy.
> The waters covered their enemies;
> There was not one of them left.
> Then they believed His words;
> They sang His praise.
> They soon forgot His works;
> They did not wait for His counsel.

Psalm 106:7–13

David exhorts us, "Bless the LORD, O my soul; and all that is within me, bless His holy name! Bless the LORD, O my soul, and forget not all His benefits" (Psalm 103:1–2). Then David names the benefits:

1. God forgives all your iniquities.
2. He heals all your diseases.
3. He redeems your life from destruction.
4. He crowns you with lovingkindness and tender mercies.
5. He satisfies your mouth with good things, so that your youth is renewed like the eagle's (see verses 3–5).

God Keeps Meticulous Records

After Jesus fed the multitudes with the mighty miracle of a few loaves and fish (you cannot slice it that thin!), He had an accurate memory of what He had done. The disciples needed some reminding later, though. One day they got in the boat and realized that they had only brought along one loaf of bread. About the same time, Jesus was exhorting them to beware of the leaven of the Pharisees and Sadducees. Hearing Him teach, they began to reason that they had not brought along enough bread. Jesus sensed what they were thinking and began to rebuke them for *not remembering* what He had accomplished previously. "Why do you reason because you have no bread? Do you not yet perceive nor understand? Is your heart still hardened? Having eyes, do you not see? And having ears, do you not hear? And do you not remember?" (Mark 8:17–18).

Jesus reminded them of His two miracles of feeding the multitudes and challenged them to remember that not only were the multitudes fed, but that many large baskets full of fragments were left over. (He not only fed them, He gave them takeout!) "When I broke the five loaves for the five thousand, how many baskets full of fragments did you take up?" With tremendous intellect, they answered, "Twelve." "Also, when I broke the seven for the four thousand, how many large baskets full of fragments did you take up?" They answered "Seven." He was indignant and asked, "How is it you do not understand?" (verses 19–21).

Jesus had just performed two mighty miracles, and yet the disciples' hearts were so hardened they still did not comprehend who He was and how sufficient He was to meet any need. Their sluggishness and dullness were no different from ours today. We so quickly doubt the power and goodness of God. How many miracles do we miss out on because we refuse to stir up our faith by not remembering what He has done previously? Clearly, human nature can quickly dismiss the wonder-working power of God and cancel out potential miracles simply because we do not remember past ones. But He is keeping records.

Take Time to Give Thanks

When Jesus healed the ten lepers who had cried out to Him for mercy, only one returned to give thanks. Jesus' response to their cry of desperation was, "Go show yourselves to the priests." By Levitical law, a priest had to declare a leper cleansed before he could go back into society. The ten obeyed Jesus, and what a sight it must have been as the horrible cancerous decay on their bodies was healed before their eyes. "So it was that as they went, they were cleansed" (Luke 17:14). What happened next is heart-warming: "And one of them, when he saw that he was healed, returned, and with a loud voice glorified God and fell down on his face at His feet, giving Him thanks. And he was a Samaritan" (verses 15–16).

The Samaritan who did give thanks was an outcast of Jewish society, which makes for even greater emphasis on his response. An outsider was the only one with a grateful heart and the courtesy to take the time to give thanks. It is appalling that only one out of ten bothered to say thank you. Jesus was keeping a record, and His response to ingratitude is still the same today: "Were there not ten cleansed? But where are the nine? Were there not any found who returned to give glory to God except this foreigner?" (verses 17–18).

Speaking of outsiders, three other people in the gospels fit into this category with the Samaritan leper. The centurion in Luke 7 made only one request for his desperately sick servant: "Say the word, and my servant will be healed." Jesus was amazed at his response. "When Jesus heard these things, He marveled at him, and turned around and said to the crowd that followed Him, 'I say to you, I have not found such great faith, not even in Israel!'" (verses 7, 9).

The woman at the well was also an outsider, a Samaritan. Yet she, too, was more receptive than most, first inquiring about worship, then going into town and telling everyone, "Come, see a Man who told me all things that I ever did. Could this be the Christ?" (John 4:29).

Another outsider was the Greek woman of Canaan who refused to be offended by Jesus' words. When she asked Him to deliver her demon-possessed daughter, He tested her three times. First, He did not answer her. Second, He said He had only been sent to the lost sheep of Israel. Third, He said that it was not good to take the children's bread and give it to the dogs. All three times, she refused to take offense. His response at seeing this was, "O woman, great is your faith! Let it be to you as you desire" (Matthew 15:28).

These four New Testament outsiders had more faith, gratitude and recognition of the power of God than the Jewish people did. So often it is the same way in the Church. As believers, we are guilty of being ungrateful for the "light" we have and the power of God we can access.

Several years ago I was visiting Yorkshire Cathedral in York, England. Pictures of the destruction that took place in 1983 were all around. A liberal Anglican bishop was being installed, and during his inauguration speech he mocked the virgin birth and other sacred events. At around one A.M. the next morning, a lightning bolt struck the exact area where he had stood. No storm had been predicted. In fact, the sky had been clear. Yet the bolt of lightning did one million pounds of damage to the cathedral. The irony of the story is that the church hierarchy called it a coincidence, but the press reported it by saying, "It sounds as if your God is trying to talk to you." Sometimes we in the Church are so complacent, lethargic and in a stupor that we cannot recognize the very hand of God in our midst.

Forgetting Our First Love

God commended the church at Ephesus for eight things they were doing right before He confronted their greatest lack:

> I know your works [1], your labor [2], your patience [3], and that you cannot bear those who are evil [4]. And you have tested those who say they are apostles and are not, and have found them liars [5]; and you have persevered [6] and have patience [7], and have labored for My name's sake and have not become weary [8].
>
> Revelation 2:2–3

But the Ephesians had forgotten the main issue—their intimacy with God, their first love! It is amazing how He tells them to remember from where they have fallen:

> Nevertheless I have this against you, that you have left your first love. Remember therefore from where you have fallen; repent and do the first works, or else I will come to you quickly and remove your lampstand from its place—unless you repent.
>
> Revelation 2:4–5

God remembers our first encounters with Him. We might not have had a lot of wisdom, but we were head over heels in love with Him. In my early years as a believer, it was common to stay up late at night with other believers and talk about the things of God, His Word and our latest experiences with

179

Him. Sadly, over time many of us drift into a platonic relationship with Him.

We have all seen couples who are newly in love. The way they gaze at each other can make you sick to your stomach. Yet if that desperate intimacy between them slips away over time, the consequences in a marriage can be severe. As a minister, I have done marriage counseling many times, and usually it comes down to this. The woman might say, "My husband is a good provider, a good father to the children, he does repairs on the house and cars and he is a good man." But then she will say, "But I have a problem. Sometimes I need someone to talk to, but he won't engage in conversation or look me in the eyes, but would rather watch television." Because of this, she is talking about getting a divorce.

Or the man will say something such as, "My wife is a good woman. She is an excellent cook, she makes our house a real home, she works a part-time job and she is a wonderful mother." But then he will say, "But I have a problem. She rarely hugs me or shows me affection." Because of this, the man is talking divorce.

We forget that God thinks in the same manner toward us. Our intimacy with Him is priority number one, and He wants us to stay in that realm of desperate intimacy with Him. If we let it slip away and do not change, the consequences are severe. God rebuked the church in Ephesus for leaving that place of intimacy. Although they worked hard and exhibited patience and perseverance, He said He would take away their lampstand because they had left that place of intimacy and lived in a platonic relationship with Him.

What Shall I Render to the Lord?

I love to read the psalms, and David's life always inspires me. God called David a man after His own heart. David had a lot of flaws, but he was a worshiper, and he was always quick to acknowledge God and thank Him for His mighty hand at work. At one point David said, "What shall I render to the LORD for all His benefits toward me? I will take up the cup of salvation, and call upon the name of the LORD. I will pay my vows to the LORD now in the presence of all His people" (Psalm 116:12–14).

We must mature past the place of asking what God can do for us and begin to pray, "How can I give back, and what can I do to bring increase to the Kingdom of God?" Let's examine our hearts and ask the Lord how we can be a blessing to the furtherance of His Kingdom! There is an old saying written on a plaque in many Christian homes: "Only one life, 'twill soon be past—only what's done for Christ will last."

In the next two chapters, we will look at the influence we can have on others and for God's Kingdom when we enjoy the freedom of assertive living.

14

Increasing Your Influence

When I was writing my first book years ago, I had invited a man and his wife to minister in the church where I was the pastor. They were very in tune with the Holy Spirit, so one afternoon I asked the elderly minister to pray with me about my book. I can still see his face today as he bowed his head briefly and prayed, probably for less than a minute. He stopped praying and looked at me. As I looked back into his wrinkled face, he said, "Steve, you are not only going to finish this book, but you are also going to write many books in your life."

That minister "saw," through the gift of the Holy Spirit, that I would write book after book. At that time, the thought of writing more than one book had never crossed my mind! Now this is my eleventh book, and I know I will write more. You know what that experience has always said to me? God is thinking about you and me in greater ways than we are thinking about ourselves!

After finishing that book and then writing two more, I commented to someone, "My books are reaching 'tens' of people." The Lord had given me fresh insights and revelations to write about, but I was having trouble getting the news out about them. The Holy Spirit showed me that I should pray for the enlargement of influence. I prayed for two years and asked many to pray with me. One day a publisher I knew in England called and told me he had a copy of one of my books on his desk. He said that with my authorization, he would like to reprint it through his publishing company. Within ten weeks of that phone call, my book was being distributed in twenty countries.

Our Influence

In chapter 9 I stated that the devil is after our two "I's"—he wants to steal our identity and stop our influence. God desires to increase our influence and effectiveness on this earth. I believe any sincere Christian would say it is his or her desire to have greater influence for the Kingdom of God. In more than three decade of ministry, the truth that stands out to me more than anything else is that God responds to our level of hunger and desire. When we are consistently hungry and passionate for the things of God, we will see Him do great things. I have witnessed this over and over again. When God's people come before Him with a sense of expectation and put a "demand" on His presence, miracles follow.

When Paul was in prison, I am sure he felt as though his influence was diminished. But obviously God's wisdom is far greater than ours, and He knew what He was doing. Had Paul been out preaching, he would have had great influence on the people in his immediate area—but he would have been too busy and distracted to write. However, in his confinement, he wrote anointed letters to various churches that comprise more than half of the New Testament. His writings have reached billions of people.

Paul made his intentions clear:

> Brethren, I do not count myself to have apprehended; but one thing I do, forgetting those things which are behind and reach-

ing forward to those things which are ahead, I press toward the goal for the prize of the upward call of God in Christ Jesus.

Philippians 3:13–14

When Paul talked about forgetting things that were behind, I do not believe he was necessarily talking about bad things. It is always tempting to stay in our comfort zone, to dwell on past victories and accomplishments rather than pursuing the greater purpose of what the Lord has next. We serve a God who thinks on far greater terms than we do.

"My thoughts are not your thoughts, nor are your ways My ways," says the LORD. "For as the heavens are higher than the earth, so are My ways higher than your ways, and My thoughts than your thoughts."

Isaiah 55:8–9

Go Tell Your Friends

When Jesus ministered to the demon-possessed man at the tomb of the Gadarenes, the man asked earnestly if he could stay with Jesus: "He who had been demon-possessed begged him that he might be with Him" (Mark 5:18). But Jesus' command was clear: "Go home to your friends, and tell them what great things the Lord has done for you, and how He has had compassion on you" (verse 19). Jesus wanted this free man to model deliverance for everyone.

God wants His Kingdom to increase and to abound, and He expects us to have a "big mouth" about all He has accomplished for us. I mentioned already that after Jesus ministered to the woman at the well, she went into town to invite everyone to come see the man she thought could be the Christ. He used the most unlikely woman to spread the good news of His appearance.

After His resurrection, when Jesus questioned Peter's love for Him, three times Jesus said, "Feed My sheep" (see

John 21). He did not say what He was going to do additionally for Peter; rather, He was speaking of how Peter could
increase His Kingdom by feeding His sheep.

When Nathaniel was introduced to Jesus, he was taken
aback by how Jesus knew him. Jesus said, "Behold, an Israelite
indeed, in whom is no deceit," and "Before Philip called you,
when you were under the fig tree, I saw you" (John 1:47–48).
Nathaniel was impressed! But Jesus said, "Because I said to
you, 'I saw you under the fig tree,' do you believe? You will see
greater things than these" (verse 50). God wants us to know
that as we follow Him, we will see greater things!

When Paul talked about the gifts of the Holy Spirit, he
used strong words. "Pursue love, and desire [covet ear-
nestly] spiritual gifts, but especially that you may prophesy"
(1 Corinthians 14:1). Our desire should be that we are fully
equipped, with all the gifts of the Spirit flowing through us
at all times.

When Paul's life on earth was nearing an end, he talked
about going to heaven, but he knew it would increase the
Kingdom if he stayed around a little longer. "For I am hard-
pressed between the two, having a desire to depart and be
with Christ, which is far better. Nevertheless to remain in
the flesh is more needful for you" (Philippians 1:23–24). His
compassion was for those who needed his influence.

I grew up in an evangelical church where I heard little about
the working power of the Holy Spirit in our lives. To this day,
it always amazes me that some Christians rarely talk about the
Lord. Instead, they tell you what is going on in their church,
how wonderful their pastor is or the progress being made on
the construction of their new building. I always want to say
to them, "But what is the Holy Spirit telling you? How is He
moving in your life?"

To paraphrase a statement I heard, "You can spend your
life any way you wish, but you only get to spend it once." The
best way to spend our lives is to give them away. Jesus told us
that the only way we will truly find our life is to surrender it.

"For whosoever desires to save his life will lose it, but whoever loses his life for My sake will find it" (Matthew 16:25). We have to forsake our own agenda and determine to give our lives away. Jesus also said, "For what profit is it to a man if he gains the whole world, and loses his own soul?" (verse 26).

Not Reaching Our Potential

Paul mentioned one man, Onesiphorus, who was a huge blessing to him. "The Lord grant mercy to the household of Onesiphorus, for he often refreshed me, and was not ashamed of my chains" (2 Timothy 1:16). Then he mentioned two men who had hindered the Gospel: "And their message will spread like cancer. Hymenaeus and Philetus are of this sort, who have strayed concerning the truth, saying that the resurrection is already past; and they overthrow the faith of some" (2 Timothy 2:17–18). He also mentioned Alexander the coppersmith, who did him much harm (see 2 Timothy 4:14).

John mentioned Demetrius, who was a blessing: "Demetrius has a good testimony from all, and from the truth itself" (3 John 12). But he also mentioned one who stood in the way: "I wrote to the church, but Diotrephes, who loves to have the preeminence among them, does not receive us" (3 John 9).

We can be a blessing to the Kingdom, a hindrance, or fall somewhere in the middle. In school there are always C students—those who do not fail, but they do not achieve high marks either. It reminds me of the church of Laodecia, about whom God said He wished they were hot rather than cold. He corrected them, saying, "As many as I love, I rebuke and chasten. Therefore be zealous and repent" (Revelation 3:19).

How disappointing it is to live with an attitude of only maintaining and never reaching for greater results. One of the greatest travesties of the Christian life is that we fall far short of the potential that God sees in us. It is said that at the end of his life, Einstein had only utilized 10 percent of his brain. Will it be said of believers on Judgment Day that only a small portion of our spiritual potential was fulfilled? As Christians, we must realize that God is thinking bigger than we are about our lives, and we need to call upon Him to bring our lives to their full potential.

Passivity is the enemy of our potential. Once we defeat this enemy, our eyes are open to see the tremendous opportunities the Spirit of God is providing for us to be a blessing in every situation. God is more than willing to take our lives to a new level of influence. The Holy Spirit is user-friendly, and once our motives change, we can see so clearly how to abide in an available state of usefulness and effectiveness.

Jesus taught a lot about fruitfulness:

> I am the vine, you are the branches. He who abides in Me, and I in him, bears much fruit; for without Me you can do nothing. . . . By this My father is glorified, that you bear much fruit; so you will be My disciples. . . . You did not choose Me, but I chose you and appointed you that you should go and bear fruit, and that your fruit should remain.
>
> John 15:5, 8, 16

In the parable of the sower, Jesus taught that we would bring forth a crop, "some a hundredfold, some sixty, some thirty" (Matthew 13:8). A hundredfold does not mean 100 percent, but rather maximum potential. God wants us individually to reach our full potential.

One undeniable attribute of God is that He is ongoing. He always desires to take us to higher and higher levels. "But we all, with unveiled face, beholding as in a mirror the glory of the Lord, are being transformed into the same image from glory to glory, just as by the Spirit of the Lord" (2 Corinthians 3:18). Each of us needs to aim higher. I find it interesting that Scripture says, "All have sinned and fall short of the glory of God" (Romans 3:23). It does not say we have come short of good teaching, a good church or a good Bible study, but rather short of the glory of God!

Room for Improvement

A Jew named Apollos had high credentials, yet he still had room for improvement:

> Now a certain Jew named Apollos, born at Alexandria, an eloquent man and mighty in the Scriptures, came to Ephesus. This man had been instructed in the way of the Lord; and being fervent in spirit, he spoke and taught accurately the things of the Lord, though he knew only the baptism of John. So he began to speak boldly in the synagogue. When Aquila and Priscilla heard him, they took him aside and explained to him the way of God more accurately.
>
> Acts 18:24–26

Maturity involves far more than putting a stop to our sin. It involves more than attending church faithfully. Maturity comes when we begin to see life from God's perspective in order to be a blessing to the Kingdom of God. Paul wrote:

> That the God of our Lord Jesus Christ, the Father of glory, may give to you the spirit of wisdom and revelation in the knowledge of Him, the eyes of your understanding being enlightened; that you may know what is the hope of His calling, what are the riches of the glory of His inheritance in the saints.
>
> Ephesians 1:17–18

Maturity comes when we begin to see by the Spirit and we stop trusting our sense realm. As believers filled with the Holy Spirit, we have a new set of eyes and a new set of ears that are located in our inner man.

189

Enlarge My Influence!

The entire Bible contains only two verses about Jabez, but they are powerful. His mother called him Jabez because she had given birth to him in much pain. So here is a man with a name meaning "he will cause pain." Can you imagine how people must have wanted to avoid him? The truth is, we have all been born into this world and caused pain. There is no greater pain causer than self-centeredness. Yet something in Jabez was not willing to stay in that place. The Bible says he was more honorable than his brothers. We can choose to aim higher in life rather than to become just another "What's in it for me?" person.

Jabez went to God with a request: "Oh, that You would bless me indeed, and enlarge my territory [borders], that Your hand would be with me, and that You would keep me from evil, that I may not cause pain!" (1 Chronicles 4:10). Jabez prayed that God would not only bless him, but that He would enlarge his territory—his influence. God granted his request. God is more than willing to take our lives to a new level of influence as well.

God answered the prayer of Jabez because it was an unselfish prayer. Jabez prayed beyond himself and asked for more territory. That must have pleased God greatly. So many prayers God hears are requests for Him to meet various needs that people have. He is truly a God who answers prayer and meets our needs, but it must be rare when someone asks Him to enlarge his or her influence for the purpose of increasing the Kingdom of God.

Many times when I visit someone in the hospital, I will make my way over to the window of the maternity ward and take a quick look at the array of newborn babies. As I scan the infant crowd, I muse whether any one of them will grow up with a desire to have an influence for the Kingdom of God—or whether they will only grow up as more self-centered people living out their lives all wrapped up in their own interests.

Sphere of Influence

Paul talked about having a sphere of influence:

> We, however, will not boast beyond measure, but within the limits of the sphere which God appointed us—a sphere which especially includes you . . . but having hope, that as your faith is increased, we shall be greatly enlarged by you in our sphere.
>
> 2 Corinthians 10:13, 15

We all have a sphere of influence, starting with our families and our co-workers. But as we pray and faithfully minister to those closest to us, God will be faithful to enlarge our sphere of influence. Many want to influence the world, but do not want to bother with those closest to them. Yet "He who is faithful in what is least is faithful also in much; and he who is unjust in what is least, is unjust also in much" (Luke 16:10).

Jesus' last words on this earth were, "But you shall receive power when the Holy Spirit has come upon you; and you shall be witnesses to Me in Jerusalem, and in all Judea and Samaria, and to the end of the earth" (Acts 1:8). When we hear the Great Commission, "Go into all the world and preach the gospel to every creature" (Mark 16:15), it helps me to think of it this way: If we have the mentality that we have to go somewhere else on the planet, we miss the point. The world is all around us. People of every race and with every kind of need are not far from any of us. All we have to do is be available to let the Holy Spirit flow through us. What about the men who let Paul down over the wall in a basket? (See Acts 9:25; 2 Corinthians 11:33.) Their names are not mentioned in the Bible, yet Paul's ministry would have halted without their help. John Maxwell said that in a normal lifetime we will have an influence on ten thousand people. How much more if we pray for God to increase His Kingdom through us?

When Orville Redenbacher asked consultants how he could get his unique popcorn business off the ground, to his amazement they told him, "The key to your success is in your name." His response was that he had always hated his name. But he took their advice, and now his popcorn is a household name in many countries. This is such a lesson to us. We do not like ourselves and often wish we were someone else. But the key to the Lord using any of us is being ourselves. God wants to anoint *us*, not a fantasy of who we would like to be!

From a City to a Country

Philip had a huge influence when he preached in the city of Samaria. The effects of his ministry were mind-boggling:

> And the multitudes with one accord heeded the things spoken by Philip, hearing and seeing the miracles which he did. For unclean spirits, crying with a loud voice, came out of many who were possessed; and many who were paralyzed and lame were healed. And there was great joy in that city.
>
> Acts 8:6–8

But his influence did not stop there! An angel of the Lord told Philip to leave the place where the Holy Spirit had done such great things and instructed him to go into the desert (Gaza). It was not until he arrived there that he heard the Lord speak to him the second time. Philip observed only one man riding on the road. The Holy Spirit instructed him to go and join the man's chariot, which he did. The interesting thing is that this time the Lord sent Philip to just one man. Yet that man was a significant vessel of great influence—an Ethiopian eunuch second in command of an entire country! Philip led the man to a knowledge of Jesus Christ, and no doubt the man influenced huge multitudes of people following his conversion (see Acts 8:26–39).

How Do I Increase My Influence?

So how do we have greater impact for the Kingdom of God? I believe we can start with simple things:

1. Pray for people on the spot. The next time someone asks for prayer, pray for him or her right then, expecting God to give you a prophetic word of encouragement to share.
2. Recognize that we are His hands and feet. God wants to use us to increase His Kingdom. Boldly seize any opportunity to tell the good news of the Gospel.
3. Be faithful in small things. Obey God in the smallest detail, and you can be assured He will give you more to do and say.
4. Be aware of the little foxes in your life. Be willing to immediately deal with the little things that try to steal your focus and attention.
5. Know your strengths. Not everything has your name on it. You are only anointed to do what God has called you to do.
6. Refuse to be stuck in fear. Refuse the fear of man and the fear of taking a risk. Be bold.
7. Protect your life from busyness. Busyness causes barrenness and will be a trap that occupies your mind and draws energy away from God's priorities.

In the following chapter, we will examine the subject of growing God's Kingdom in more depth. His Kingdom, not ours, is being increased on the earth. It is not about us, but about Him.

15

Growing God's Kingdom

Last year a friend asked if I could advise him on where he could attend church. I recommended a church that I thought he would enjoy. A few months later, he told me that he had attended that church fourteen Sundays in a row, and no one had spoken to him or reached out to him. Ironically, this church greatly emphasizes evangelism and has a vision for reaching out to the community. However, when my friend attended the services, the people all talked to one another and completely ignored him—a visitor. This reminds me so much of Jesus' statement, "For if you love those who love you, what reward have you? Do not even the tax collectors do the same? And if you greet your brethren only, what do you do more than others?" (Matthew 5:46–47). God is not impressed when our friendliness only reaches to those who love us.

Through this incident I began to meditate on how we can be so blind to the needs of people around us. It is funny how characteristic this is of many sincere believers. In one sense we want to influence the world, but in another sense we are so self-centered that we cannot be compassionate and sensitive in our immediate surroundings. If our Christianity does not affect those in close proximity to us, just how real is it? Jesus made it plain: "The Son of Man did not come to be served, but to serve, and to give His life a ransom for many" (Matthew 20:28). But the prevailing self-centered attitude says to the Lord, "What have You done for me lately?"

You Are a Rembrandt!

Around 1999, a man shopping at a flea market purchased a painting for twenty dollars. Examining the painting, he thought it was unusual and unique, so he took it to some professionals, who informed him there was another painting underneath its surface. They meticulously removed the outer painting and discovered that the original painting underneath was done by the famous artist Rembrandt. A couple of years later, the buyer was interviewed on the *Today* show. He said his surprise purchase had sold at a 2001 Christie's auction in London for 1.4 million dollars! He made a good profit after subtracting the twenty dollars.

When I heard this amazing story, I sensed that the Holy Spirit was showing me how that painting exactly represents the state of the believer in Christ. When God saves our souls, He puts a "Rembrandt" (the authentic Holy Spirit) within us. This "treasure in earthen vessels" is what the Christian life is all about—"If anyone is in Christ, he is a new creation" (2 Corinthians 4:7; 5:17).

We are new, and our inner man is perfect and pure. The problem is that we have another painting on top of us—the old nature, our flesh. The old painting's materials are our wounds, experiences of rejection and low self-worth. As the Holy Spirit works with us, He removes that old nature, and little by little the true "Rembrandt" is revealed—the new creation in Christ. The Holy Spirit's work in us (sanctification) is not accomplished by making us something He wants us to be, but by stripping away the flesh ("grave clothes" of a sort) to reveal who we already are in Christ.

Think about when Jesus raised Lazarus from the dead. Although Lazarus was resurrected, he still had a great need that Jesus addressed as He commanded the disciples, "Loose him, and let him go" (John 11:44). Although we have been made alive in Christ, we can still be wearing the "grave clothes" of old thinking patterns and wounds from our past. The truth is, we are worthwhile because we have been made in God's image.

I understood later that with the story of the painting, the Holy Spirit was showing me that God does not have confidence in us—His confidence is in the Holy Spirit (the Rembrandt)—the treasure He has placed within us. No wonder God tells us, "He who has begun a good work in you will complete it until the day of Jesus Christ" (Philippians 1:6).

Treasure in Styrofoam Cups

God knew what He was doing when He chose us. Seeing our flaws and inconsistencies does not catch Him off guard. He took a risk when He placed the Holy Spirit in our flawed but redeemed personalities. He chooses to be glorified by revealing His power through us. We are simply the vessels He uses—the Styrofoam cups.

> For it is the God who commanded light to shine out of darkness, who has shone in our hearts to give the light of the knowledge of the glory of God in the face of Jesus Christ. But we have this treasure in earthen vessels, that the excellence of the power may be of God and not of us.
>
> 2 Corinthians 4:6–7

We live in a needy world, and we do not have to look far to find someone with a need. Personally, I wish I had never spent so many hours over the years praying about my weaknesses and problems. Now, finally, I can see the obvious—that I am just the human earthen vessel, the Styrofoam cup, and God has placed the treasure, the Holy Spirit, within me. What a waste of time to pray about the weaknesses of my flesh. Sure, it is good to ask God for strength to overcome, but it is far more effective to concentrate on the treasure within us—the precious and powerful Holy Spirit. The more we exalt and acknowledge Him, the more we lose interest in listing all of our shortcomings and the pulls of the fleshly nature.

The Holy Spirit Is for Everyone

During my first years in ministry, I woke up one morning to hear the Holy Spirit speaking two sentences to me with extreme clarity. He said, *Those looking to heaven are missing it. I'm looking for those who have the living water flowing through them.*

If heaven is our aim, we are missing it! Many times we are looking for a way to escape this world, but God is trying to get *into* this world through us. He wants everyone who comes across our path to be touched by the Holy Spirit within us. When He gave us the Holy Spirit, He was not thinking of us per se, but of everyone whom He would bring across our paths.

I love animals, and their behavior amuses me. If you own a dog and feed it and take care of it, you can almost read the dog's mind saying to you, *You must be a god.* But if you own a cat and feed it and take care of it, you can easily read its mind: *I must be a god.* As the saying goes, "Dogs have masters, but cats have staff."

Many people have the cat mentality. As they experience the blessings and goodness of God, they in effect say, "I must be the priority here." But the Gospel is not about us and our agenda and comfort; it is about Him! If we try to hold on to our lives, we will actually lose them, but in giving them away for His sake, we will find them (see Matthew 16:25). Even in the Lord's Prayer, it is all about His Kingdom: "Your Kingdom come. Your will be done . . ." (Matthew 6:10). It is not about our kingdom!

What Do You Have?

An Israelite widow was in trouble. Her husband, who once had an effective ministry, was dead. She was left in severe financial trouble, so severe that she approached the prophet Elisha about it. "Your servant my husband is dead, and you know that your servant feared the LORD. And the creditor is coming to take my two sons to be his slaves" (2 Kings 4:1).

The prophet's reply to her is key. His emphasis was clearly not that he should come to her rescue. Rather, his question was about what she already had: "What shall I do for you? Tell me, what do you have in the house?"

She replied, "Your maidservant has nothing in the house but a jar of oil" (verse 2). Her emphasis was on the nothing.

So often our emphasis is on our nothing, too, instead of on recognizing that we have the power of the Holy Spirit within us. Faced with difficulties, we say, "I have nothing in the house except a jar of oil." Maybe like her, we say (possibly with false humility), "I have nothing in me." How often we are guilty of being slow to acknowledge the fact that the wonderful Holy Spirit (the jar of oil) lives within us and that we have such access to His power—"according to the power that works in us" (Ephesians 3:20). We forget that Scripture explicitly states, "But he who is joined to the Lord is one spirit with Him" and that we are "joint heirs with Christ" (1 Corinthians 6:17; Romans 8:17).

The prophet's command was clear: "Go, borrow vessels from everywhere, from all your neighbors—empty vessels; do not gather just a few" (2 Kings 4:3). The prophet was freeing her from her captivity by telling her to find vessels to pour into and use the oil that she had within her house. Then he told her to close the door along with her sons and begin to pour her oil into the empty vessels. He exhorted her not to gather just a few. It was time to get radical, to think big and give out of her need.

When the widow finally ran out of empty vessels, the oil stopped flowing: "Now it came to pass, when the vessels were full, that she said to her son, 'Bring me another vessel.' And he said to her, 'There is not another vessel.' So the oil ceased" (verse 6). Taking her story as an illustration, it seems as though what makes the oil stop flowing in our lives is when we stop pouring out into empty vessels.

Is God talking to you the same way Elisha talked to the widow? You might say that you have so many needs, but God replies to you, *What do you have in your life?* You have the Holy Spirit (the jar of oil), and now you need to look for empty vessels to pour into. You do not have to look far to find someone with a need (an empty vessel) who could use a word of encouragement. You can start right now by pouring into his or her life. As you do, God will take care of your needs. "Seek first the kingdom of God and His righteousness, and all these things shall be added to you" (Matthew 6:33).

How Can I Find Empty Vessels?

The prophet challenged this widow the same way the Holy Spirit challenges us. She had to follow Elisha's counsel to act assertively and take action to improve her situation. Rather than being stuck in passivity, we can take action, as she did—action that leads to life-changing experiences. We just need to take our minds off of ourselves and find empty vessels to pour into. And as we do that, God pours into us. Here are some good ways to find and pour into empty vessels:

1. Ask the Lord to show you a person to pray for. Take twenty or thirty minutes to pray for that person, and record any encouragement the Holy Spirit shares regarding him or her. Then tell that person.
2. When someone tells you of a need, stop right then and pray in faith with that person, joining in expectation that the Lord will meet that need.
3. If you know someone who has a financial need, help meet it if you can. Even a small amount is an encouraging gesture.
4. Ask someone who might not be noticed by others to coffee or lunch and have a conversation that encourages him or her. Do not take your best friend along!
5. Tell someone how he or she has blessed your life or how you have noticed the things he or she does.
6. Remind someone of the strengths you see in him or her.
7. If you are a woman, offer a few hours of free day care to a single mom.
8. If you are a man, offer to take a single mom's son fishing.
9. Offer to get the oil changed in a single mom's or a widow's car.
10. Ask the Lord for someone He might want you to mentor. You can begin by merely being a good listener. The Lord will make a way for you to "pour" into that person until he or she becomes stronger and more fit for the Master's use.

God Will Pay You Back!

A prominent and influential woman from Shunem passionately desired to be a blessing. She said to her husband one day:

> Look now, I know that this is a holy man of God, who passes by us regularly. Please, let us make a small upper room on the wall; and let us put a bed for him there, and a table and a chair and a lampstand; so it will be, whenever he comes to us, he can turn in there.
>
> 2 Kings 4:9–10

This woman had an unselfish vision to minister to the prophet. She blessed his life with a place to stay and rest. One day the prophet made an unusual request of her. He told his servant to say these words to her: "Look, you have been concerned for us with all this care. What can I do for you?" (verse 13).

Can you imagine God in heaven watching you blessing His Kingdom, and then having Him say, "What can I do for you?" At first Elisha was frustrated because when he tried to bless her, even offering to speak to the king on her behalf, she claimed she did not have any need. She replied, "I dwell among my own people."

Finally Gehazi, his servant, told the prophet about a need she had—"Actually, she has no son, and her husband is old."

The prophet called her again and gave her an awesome message: "About this time next year you shall embrace a son."

Her response was emotional. "No, my lord. Man of God, do not lie to your maidservant!" (verses 13–14, 16).

I believe the prophet addressed her greatest hope and desire, which she had already given up on. No doubt she had prayed for a child for years, but it had never happened. The prophet's news was so great that she did not want him to get her hopes up again. Maybe there is also an unfulfilled desire that has never come to pass in your life that God will grant. If you concentrate on God's business, looking for ways to bless His Kingdom and do the possible, then He will do the impossible!

God is very generous. Peter said to Jesus one day, "We have left all and followed You" (Mark 10:28). Jesus' reply was amazing:

Assuredly, I say to you, there is no one who has left house or brothers or sisters or father or mother or wife or children or lands, for My sake and the gospel's, who shall not receive a hundredfold now in this time—houses and brothers and sisters and mothers and children and lands, with persecutions—and in the age to come, eternal life.

Mark 10:29–30

In the next chapter, we will look at some areas that provide structure for our own spiritual growth as we desire the growth of God's Kingdom and as we work to see it happen.

16

Working Out Your Own Salvation

When I was fourteen, my father agreed to let me purchase an antique 1930 Model A Ford pickup. It was in poor shape and did not run, plus it had a lot of rust and numerous missing parts. But for fifty dollars I became the new owner. I was so proud of that old truck. It took me twenty years to fix it up, seeking help from many friends and professionals. I ended up dismantling it down to every bolt and piece of sheet metal. I had the frame sandblasted, I located and installed replacement parts, I rebuilt the engine and a multitude of other pieces and I painstakingly put it back together. But when I was 34, I finished my project. What a sight it was! It looked showroom new and boasted beautiful, dark Brewster green paint, and it had shiny black fenders and yellow spoke wheels. I even got a personalized license plate—"An Old 1."

Although I was officially the owner at fourteen, I still needed to restore the old, rusty pickup truck and return it to its original condition. What a clear picture this is of our salvation. When we finally surrender our lives to Jesus Christ, repent of our sins and begin to follow Him, we are under new ownership. But that is just the beginning. God wants to "restore" us, healing deep-rooted rejection, damaged emotions, fears and inherited traits. He wants to bring us to maturity and wholeness. The good news of the Gospel is that we have been forgiven and redeemed by His blood, and now He begins the process of restoration in us. But we have to work with God and be willing to honestly face things as He puts His touch on areas that need work.

How does this relate to passivity? In countless ways! Many people expect someone else to take responsibility for their lives. The epitome of sin, starting with Adam, is the refusal to take responsibility. At the first evidence of sin, God confronted Adam with "Have you eaten from the tree of which I commanded you that you should not eat?" Adam took no responsibility for his actions, but instead blamed God and Eve for his disobedience: "The woman whom You gave to be with me, she gave me of the tree, and I ate" (Genesis 3:11–12).

As we face our passive and aggressive behavior, we recognize that God limits Himself according to our willingness to cooperate with His Holy Spirit. As I said at the start, being a Christian is not enough; reading the Bible, praying and even regular church attendance are not enough. I have said for years that churches are great places to hide from God! It is not enough to look as if we have it together but be living without a fervent heart, unplugged from God. Again, "The backslider in heart will be filled with his own ways" (Proverbs 14:14).

We must have a passionate willingness to allow God to change us. When we realize that we are responsible for our own lives, we can assertively decide to walk with God into healing and wholeness. God is committed to each of us! "He who has begun a good work in you will complete it until the day of Jesus Christ" (Philippians 1:6).

In other words, God has decided that He will work in our lives all the way to the end. How we choose to let Him put His finger on areas of our lives will determine our destiny, our freedom and our ultimate happiness. God has an agenda—to perfect us and conform us into His image. "For whom He foreknew, He also predestined to be conformed to the image of His Son" (Romans 8:29). Although the blood of Jesus has cleansed us from sin, the work of the Holy Spirit restores our souls, cleanses us of wrong motives and delivers us from self-centeredness, until we are living a life devoted to the increase of the Kingdom of God.

So then, what is our part? We have to join with God in this endeavor. We have to work out our own salvation with fear and trembling (see Philippians 2:12). Just as a coach works with an athlete to perfect his skills, so, too, the Holy Spirit works individually with each of us to point out areas where we need to respond to Him. Like a coach, God tells us to work on our game. The writer of Hebrews declares, "It is a fearful [terrible] thing to fall into the hands of the living God" (Hebrews 10:31).

One meaning of the word *sin* is "to miss the mark." In America, polls say that 85 percent of people believe in God— but believing He exists does not constitute a life committed to Him. Jesus said of the Pharisees, "This people honors Me with their lips, but their heart is far from Me" (Mark 7:6). James said, "You believe that there is one God. You do well. Even the demons believe—and tremble!" (James 2:19). For a while, a popular saying went around in Christian circles: "If you were arrested for being a Christian, would there be enough evidence to convict you?" If our lives are to give evidence of living for the Kingdom, we need to take note of five areas:

1. We must recognize that we alone are responsible for ourselves.
2. We must learn to get control of our mouths.
3. We must be on guard against self-deception.
4. We must learn to cooperate with the Holy Spirit.
5. We must recognize that faith is not what we believe, but what we do.

207

You Are Responsible for You

It is tempting to see ourselves as victims or to compare ourselves with other people and say, "At least I'm not like them" or "I wish I were more like them and had what they have." Peter did it. At one point Jesus spoke to Peter prophetically, "Most assuredly, I say to you, when you were younger, you girded yourself and walked where you wished; but when you are old, you will stretch out your hands, and another will gird you and carry you where you do not wish" (John 21:18). Peter's immediate response was to point to the disciple John and say, "What about this man?"

Jesus was indignant: "If I will that he remain till I come, what is that to you?" (verse 22). He was telling Peter to mind his own business and recognize that he was only responsible for his life—not John's. Along those lines, Paul said, "But they, measuring themselves by themselves, and comparing themselves among themselves, are not wise" (2 Corinthians 10:12).

When each of us stands before God at the Judgment, we will not have someone standing there with us on whom we can place the blame. We alone will answer to God for how we let Him work with us and how we worked out our own salvation. It is to the glory of God that we ask the Lord now to uproot anything in our lives that is not pleasing to Him. David said, "Search me, O God, and know my heart; try me . . . and see if there is any wicked way in me, and lead me in the way everlasting" (Psalm 139:23–24).

Controlling Your Mouth

Needing tires for my car, I approached the mechanic whom I trusted and did business with regularly. He put four new tires on my car and told me they would last for forty thousand miles. However, less than a year later I went in for an oil change and he informed me that my tires were worn out.

I was livid, and I reminded him of his promise that the tires would last a long time. He quickly pointed out to me that the problem was not with the tires he had sold me, but that I had allowed the car to get so far out of alignment that it had worn out the tires. It was an expensive lesson. Just think how many times we blame God for things when the real problem is that we are out of alignment with His purpose and are wearing ourselves out.

Sometimes we create our own problems with our mouths. As our mouths go, so go our lives. Following his exhortation to "work out your own salvation," Paul wrote, "Do all things without complaining and disputing" (Philippians 2:12, 14). We must get a firm grip on our words, recognizing that "death and life are in the power of the tongue" (Proverbs 18:21). God rebuked the Israelites, fed up with the continual complaining that came out of their mouths: "How long shall I bear with this evil congregation who complain against Me?" (Numbers 14:27). And James wrote, "If anyone among you thinks he is religious, and does not bridle his tongue but deceives his own heart, this one's religion is useless" (James 1:26).

The rudder on a ship may weigh only a few hundred pounds, but it guides a huge vessel that may weigh 170,000 tons. Likewise, James also tells us that although the tongue is a small organ, it can guide the course of our lives for good or ill.

> Look also at ships: although they are so large and are driven by fierce winds, they are turned by a very small rudder wherever the pilot desires. Even so the tongue is a little member and boasts great things.
>
> James 3:4–5

When we passively engage in speaking negative words full of self-hatred or blame, we are not in agreement with God. The bottom line is that we have to say about ourselves what

God says about us—we are forgiven, redeemed, new creations, more than conquerors, oaks of righteousness and set free.

Beware of Self-Deception

There is no greater deception than self-deception. People have always lied to themselves and lied to God. We have difficulty seeing ourselves as we really are, and it is so easy to lie to ourselves about it. It is almost like having a blind spot in traffic. You were sure no one was there when you began to change lanes. Then you heard someone honking and had to swerve back into your lane. Every person thinks his own perspective is accurate and is quick to express his opinion, but James exhorts us by saying, "But be doers of the word, and not hearers only, deceiving yourselves" (James 1:22). It seems so easy to see errors in someone else but not in ourselves. We all have blind spots, and only God can keep our coast clear for us.

One of the Scriptures most pertinent to our society is, "Woe to those who call evil good, and good evil; who put darkness for light, and light for darkness; who put bitter for sweet, and sweet for bitter!" (Isaiah 5:20). Popular talk shows will scorn good values and cheer perversion. The devil is a deceiver. Because he is already defeated, he does not and cannot operate through power. Jesus said, "All power has been given unto Me." So what does that leave the devil? Satan can only operate through deception. People are deceived by listening to lies.

When we receive the Holy Spirit, we receive the Spirit of Truth. It is the truth that sets us free. "If you abide [continue] in My word, you are my disciples indeed. And you shall know the truth, and the truth shall make you free" (John 8:31–32). Truth takes root as we are proactive in our pursuit of God.

Passive people often refuse to work out their own salvation. They refuse to actively resist lies, when as believers we need to aggressively challenge every lie. A friend of mine says, "A lie unchallenged becomes the truth you live by." Paul wrote about some people in the last days who lived according to unchallenged lies. He commented that they had a form of godliness but denied its power, and he said, "From such people turn away!" (2 Timothy 3:5). He also warned us of this day, "But evil men and impostors will grow worse and worse, deceiving and being deceived" (verse 13). For example, today it is more and more common to hear of unmarried Christian couples living together with no effect on their consciences. They are living a lie. Such practices are nothing but self-deception—the Word of God has not changed (see 1 Corinthians 6:9–10).

I like to say that it is not how you start, it is how you finish. It does not matter how well you start a race or an athletic event—the final outcome is what matters. So, too, God wants us to follow Him until we can celebrate a good finish. Paul said, "I have fought the good fight, I have finished the race, I have kept the faith" (2 Timothy 4:7).

Cooperate with the Holy Spirit

When Jesus left the earth, He did something wonderful— He left the Holy Spirit in charge. The Holy Spirit is on the earth to help us and guide us daily. He is here to lead us into all truth. Jesus explained to His disciples that it was to their advantage that He left:

> Nevertheless I tell you the truth. It is to your advantage that I go away; for if I do not go away, the Helper will not come to you; but if I depart, I will send Him to you. . . . However, when He, the Spirit of truth, has come, He will guide you into all truth; for He will not speak on His own authority, but whatever He hears He will speak; and He will tell you things to come.
>
> John 16:7, 13

I believe that the Holy Spirit is the most underused and underaccessed Person in the universe. But He is here to help us! Many times I ask the Holy Spirit questions regarding issues I face. One day, I asked Him why I had such a problem with indecision. Immediately He spoke to my spirit, *Indecision is rooted in pride. You are afraid of making a wrong decision because you are trying to protect your pride, so you don't make any decision.* Although that was not necessarily what I wanted to hear, it was the truth. As I embraced it, I was set free.

If the Lord has given you a prophetic word, stand on what He said. Remind Him of the promise, and as Paul told Timothy, "This charge I commit to you, son Timothy, according to the prophecies previously made concerning you, that by them you may wage the good warfare" (1 Timothy 1:18). When the Lord told Elijah He was going to send rain on the earth, Elijah cooperated and went up on top of Mount Carmel and prayed for rain. He locked himself into agreement with the word of the Lord (see 1 Kings 18).

Faith Is What You Do

Faith is action. I like to ask people, "Do you believe in exercise and that it is good for your health?" Most people agree that it is. Then I ask, "Do you exercise daily?" Usually their answer is no. In other words, they believe a truth without living the truth. That is the problem for many of us. We have a belief system but are not living it out in our lifestyle. James addressed the issue this way: "Thus also, faith by itself, if it does not have works [corresponding action], is dead" (James 2:17).

If you make an appointment with a doctor and he examines you and hands you a prescription, how foolish it would be to throw it in the wastebasket on your way out the door. No, you must take action, going to the pharmacy and having the prescription filled. The Holy Spirit is always handing us those pieces of paper, His prescriptions telling us what we need to let Him work on in our lives. If we are passive, we do not take Him seriously and toss His instructions aside.

It is not enough to hear the Gospel; we have to act on it and let our faith ignite with what is said. "For indeed the gospel was preached to us as well as to them, but the word which they heard did not profit them, not being mixed with faith in those who heard it" (Hebrews 4:2). I like to say that you cannot get strong by watching someone else exercise!

Faith is not what we believe; it is what we do. When four men lowered a sick man down through the roof in front of Jesus, He saw their faith and healed the man (see Mark 2:1–12). Their faith involved an act so desperate that they removed roof tiles to get to the Lord.

As the disciples chose to work with the Lord, He worked with them.

> So then, after the Lord had spoken to them, He was received up into heaven, and sat down at the right hand of God. And they went out and preached everywhere, the Lord working with them and confirming the word through the accompanying signs.
>
> Mark 16:19–20

The Lord desperately desires to work with us, but we must step out in faith and start acting on what we believe. It is said that along those lines the great evangelist John Wesley commented, "Beware of asking God to do what He is expecting you to do yourself." Make a decision to work out your own salvation. Then let's see what God will do!

Conclusion

Ahab in Recovery

I confess, I was the poster child for Ahab-like passivity. Learning to live with self-respect and be assertive in word and deed has been a hard road. And I am still a work in progress. Every day, it is a challenge for me to act with assertiveness, choose to respect myself and remind myself that I am not a victim and that no person defines me—my identity is in Christ.

Why do we end up as passive people? Aside from the emotional and mental aspects we have talked about, this also is a spiritual problem. Passivity is a spirit that blinds us and cripples not only our relationships, but our effectiveness as believers. We have to take authority over this passive spirit and ask the Holy Spirit to deliver us. And we have to repent of unbelief and agree with what God says about us in His Word. He not only accepts us, He justifies us and declares us righteous through what Jesus accomplished on the cross. If we believe the lie that we are unworthy, this sets us up to try to earn love. We think, *If I don't please this person, I run the risk of being rejected or abandoned.* And rejection is our greatest fear. We wrongly think that a person we are in any type of relationship with will leave us if we do not please him or her.

A Good Formula for Recovery

As a person healed in Christ, I realize that my value is inherent. God created me with an inborn value that He placed on my life. Because of the enemy's lies and judgments from other people, the root of rejection became a stronghold in me. Now I have found this simple formula to follow to break free and get healthy.

1. *As a whole and responsible person, I realize that if I feel someone has rejected me or blamed me for something, I should take a look at the issues and ask the Holy Spirit to reveal to me what I did wrong.* I can ask myself these questions: "What is my responsibility here? Did I do something to wrong this person?" If so, I need to put pride aside, apologize and ask for forgiveness. However, if the Spirit does not show me any wrongdoing on my part, then without making accusations, I need to assertively tell the other person what my feelings are concerning his or her actions.

2. *Once I have responded assertively, I realize it is up to the other person to choose how to respond to me.* If he or she responds with defensiveness or without repentance, then I have to recognize that I cannot change another person—I can only change me. I have to realize that even though the person is rejecting me, that does not detract from my value. I breathe in and out and let it go.

Learn to picture yourself doing that very thing. Refuse to carry the incident or dwell on it anymore. If you keep carrying it, it will lead to bitterness and unforgiveness. Letting it go does not mean what another person did was right, but it means I am choosing to be free from the effects of his or her behavior and choices. If the person chooses to respond in a positive manner, then the disagreement is healed and our relationship is even stronger because we have engaged in healthy communication. If the person responds negatively and continues to attack me, then I simply recognize it as that person's problem—not mine.

3. *I pray and ask the Lord what my triggers are.* For example, feeling rejected often triggers things. However, once we trace a trigger back to rejection or the reason it caused us pain, we can address the situation assertively. We can acknowledge its source and face it with stable emotions and behavior. Sometimes someone else's words or actions trigger the pain of old wounds, and suddenly our peace is disturbed and we do not even understand why. Since we have already come to a place of healing, peace and stability in our emotions, we need to investigate right then why something disturbed our peace. We can ask the Lord to show us the root. Then we can quickly address the issue, whether it is rejection, fear, anger, an old wound or something else the Spirit shows us.

4. *I recognize that in the past, the enemy has kept me in the bondage of reactivity. I have fallen into patterns of reacting to old wounds, feeling rejection and feeling abandoned. These patterns lead to worry, anxiety and any number of familiar negative emotions.* A typical reaction to those unpleasant emotions is to attack the person involved or blame and loathe ourselves—or put into operation any one of those defense mechanisms from chapter 8. One thing that helped me simplify this whole issue of pain is recognizing that there are really only two original emotions on this earth—fear and love. All negative emotions stem from and can be traced back to fear (fear of abandonment, fear of rejection, fear of lack, fear of pain). David said, "I sought the LORD, and He heard me, and delivered me from *all* of my fears" (Psalm 34:4, emphasis added). I might add here that anger, even though it is related to fear, can be a healthy emotion. "Be angry, and do not sin" (Ephesians 4:26). Anger is a gift from God that

can help us be assertive and keep us from being abused and walked on.

We can examine ourselves each time we react to a situation, a person's behavior or someone's words. Are we responding in fear or in love? It always boils down to one or the other. Think about Elijah. He was functioning in love for God when he killed the 450 prophets of Baal who were the work of Jezebel. Yet when she threatened his life, he reacted with fear and ran from her.

Another thing that has helped me is recognizing that our reactions to the behavior of others is based on our (limited) perception of those people. We do not know what their circumstances are, and because of our own life experiences, we interpret everything through our own paradigm and belief system. For example, we might perceive a look someone gives us as a dirty look. However, that person might be facing some difficult circumstances. We are so self-absorbed that we feel the person's expression has something to do with us, when really it does not. Maybe because we are so preoccupied with ourselves, we assume everyone else is preoccupied with us, too. Again, our perception is too limited to know what is going on inside another person.

Basic Human Rights

God has given each of us a wonderful, inherent value. Sometimes when speaking to groups, I hold up a twenty-dollar bill and ask the audience how much it is worth. Everyone agrees it is worth twenty dollars. Then I wad it up and stomp on it several times. I ask everyone, "How much is it worth now?" Everyone agrees that it is still worth twenty dollars. The point is that no matter what you have been through, your value has not changed.

Speaking of value, I like these definitions of each person's human rights. It is helpful to take a moment and examine whether or not we are living passively by looking at this list of human rights. Do not expect that these are extended automatically; those with a Jezebel spirit rarely extend you these rights. You must assertively stand up and claim them for yourself.

1. Each person has the right to be treated respectfully.
2. Each person has the right to say no without explanation and without guilt.
3. Each person has the right to slow down and take time to think.
4. Each person has the right to change his or her mind.
5. Each person has the right to ask for what he or she wants.
6. Each person has the right to ask for information.
7. Each person has the right to make mistakes.
8. Each person has the right to make choices and accept the consequences of those choices.
9. Each person has the right to own and express his or her feelings.
10. Each person has the right to ask for help.
11. Each person has the right to maintain a separate self that is accountable to God and independent of the expectations, approval or influence of others.[1]

Finally, we must determine that we will not tolerate those who try to take away our power. If you or I have a propensity to take the easy road of passivity, we need to heed the warning and rebuke from the Lord given in Revelation 2:20:

> I have a few things against you, because you allow that woman Jezebel, who calls herself a prophetess, to teach and seduce My servants to commit sexual immorality and eat things sacrificed to idols.

1. Koch and Haugk, 199–200.

Whether you are a husband or a wife who is afraid to assertively believe in your own dignity as a human being, a pastor who struggles with the fear of telling people the truth or a man who has capitulated under the stronghold of pornography and sexual addiction authored by the spirit of Jezebel, it is up to you to obey the Holy Spirit and refuse to tolerate Jezebel in your life anymore.

Courage for a Changed Life!

It takes courage to invite the Holy Spirit to examine and heal our minds, our hearts and our lives. It takes courage to allow the light of the Holy Spirit to delve deeply within us to reveal the truth, and it takes courage to willingly acknowledge the truth and allow God's transforming power to change us from the inside out. The beautiful result of such courage is a changed life filled with victory and freedom—not only for you and me but for generations to come!

From generation to generation we are born into this world and into a set of behaviors and thinking patterns that are indoctrinated into us from birth. If we do not allow God to transform us, we then teach our children our same dysfunctional beliefs, behaviors and defense mechanisms. We also risk opening the door to the influence of demonic spirits that want us and our families to live in bondage to Ahab-like passivity or Jezebel-like aggression.

We have the power to stand up with courage and say, "I will be the one!"

I will be the one in my family line who will break generational curses and change the course of history and the legacy for this generation, and my children, and my children's children. How about you?

Steve Sampson is a gifted writer and effective minister who has provided thought-provoking insights to the Body of Christ about the ministry of the Holy Spirit. Characterized as a Christian Bob Newhart, his unique wit combines candor and transparency while refreshing the soul of the hearer.

Through the prophetic gifts of the Holy Spirit, Steve has ministered to people for decades by speaking personal vision, hope and expectation into their lives. Demonstrating how the Holy Spirit speaks to people, he has been a source of encouragement to others to do the same.

Steve has written a number of books, some of which are *Confronting Jezebel: Discerning and Defeating the Spirit of Control, You Can Hear the Voice of God, Those Who Expect Nothing Are Never Disappointed, Don't Talk To Me Now, Lord . . . I'm Trying To Pray* and *I Was Always on My Mind*.

You can contact Steve about ministry events and available teaching resources at:

Steve Sampson Ministries
P.O. Box 36324
Birmingham, Alabama 35236

www.stevesampson.com